MADNESS IN

PERIBAÑEZ
AND THE COMENDADOR OF OCAÑA

Lope de Vega

MADNESS IN VALENCIA

in a new version by David Johnston

PERIBAÑEZ
AND THE COMENDADOR OF OCAÑA

in a new version by Nick Drake

OBERON BOOKS
LONDON

WWW.OBERONBOOKS.COM

First published in 1998 by Oberon Books Ltd
521 Caledonian Road, London N7 9RH
Tel: +44 (0) 20 7607 3637 / Fax: +44 (0) 20 7607 3629
e-mail: info@oberonbooks.com
www.oberonbooks.com

British Library cataloguing-in-publication data
A catalogue record for this book is available from the British Library.

ISBN: 978-0-94823-066-0

Visit www.oberonbooks.com to read more about all our books and to buy
them. You will also find features, author interviews and news of any author
events, and you can sign up for e-newsletters so that you're always first to
hear about our new releases.

Contents

MADNESS IN VALENCIA

Introduction

Confusion, in the most chaotically positive sense of the word, might be said to sum up the essence of the life, art, (and of course times) of Lope Félix de Vega Carpio (1562-1635). The details of his restless and flamboyant lifestyle have been recounted *ad nauseam* in biographies, commentaries and introductions such as this. What emerges from that collision of wives and mistresses, births and deaths, arms and letters that was his life is an omnipresent, albeit characteristically enigmatic and elusive, cultural labyrinth. There are few aspects of life and letters in the Spain of his day in which he does not play a part. His roles are varied, his masks often assumed simultaneously: soldier (he was a volunteer on the *Armada Invencible* of 1588), priest (he took holy orders in 1614 after the deaths of his second wife and favourite son Carlos), court sycophant (he served the Duke of Alba from 1590, was secretary to the Marqués de Malpica and the Conde de Lemos, and from 1605 was responsible for the Duke of Sessa's correspondence), philanderer (two wives and three affairs that we can be sure of) and, of course, prolific literary genius.

Although best remembered in literature as a dramatist and creator of a new National Theatre, Lope published works in all the fashionable genres. He wrote a pastoral novel, the *Arcadia* (1598); epics such as *La Dragontea* (1598) and *La Jerusalén conquistada* (*Jerusalem Reconquered*, 1609); and prose works like *El peregrino en su patria* (*The Pilgrim in his Homeland*, 1604). In an attempt to assail the vernacular poetic canon he embraced the Petrarchan muse which had been so successfully appropriated by his Spanish predecessor Garcilaso de la Vega almost a century earlier. The result was the secular lyrical collection *Rimas* (*Rhymes*), published in 1602, in which two hundred sonnets first appeared in print. However, neither life nor art had a Daedalian middle way for Lope de Vega, and although he had already penned the religious epic *El Isidro* in 1599, it was with the publication of the *Rimas sacras* (*Sacred Rhymes*) in 1614 that, as poet/priest, he soared to new, if ambivalent, mystical heights. Both his amorous and mystical literary fires, however, were to be well and truly extinguished twenty years later when his lyrical work turned to explore the earthy depths of the burlesque. In his *Rimas humanas y divinas,* (*Human and Divine Rhymes*, 1634) a lifetime's expression of poeticised carnal and spiritual fervour was mercilessly parodied by his alter-ego Tomé de Burguillos.

On a different, though related stage, Lope de Vega was one of the main protagonists in the literary controversies of his day. Indeed we could go as far as to say that he had an innate talent for inciting and directing the polemic in which he starred. His ironic treatise about the new art of writing plays, *El arte nuevo de hacer comedias en este tiempo* (published in 1609; see *Lope de Vega: Two Plays*, Absolute Classics, 1992), gave rise to a number of commentaries on drama in Spain, some favouring his "new art" innovations, others attacking what they saw as dangerously flawed commercial and formulaic theatre which prioritised "gusto" (public taste) at the expense of art. The major literary debate of the early seventeenth century, however, focused less on the "new art" of Lope's drama and more on the "new poetry" inspired by Luis de Góngora's ground-breaking *Polifemo* (*Polyphemus*) and *Soledades* (*Solitudes*).

To be "culto" or not to be "culto" was the burning question which divided the *literati* of the day. If we understand "culto" as referring to a sort of stylistic baroqueness, then we can say that Lope championed the cause of those anti-Gongorine poets who preferred conceptual clarity to linguistic obscurity. In retrospect it is clear that we cannot talk about two schools of literature, but two approaches to writing with shifts in emphasis dividing them; most significantly the *res verba* struggle for pre-eminence. Once the vitriolic polemic got under way, however, it acquired a momentum all of its own, and Lope himself was the target of a bitter attack on his work, the *Spongia*, published in 1617. His supporters (perhaps with the support of Lope) answered with the *Expostulatio Spongiae* (1618). In fact when Lope published volume 13 of his *comedias* in Madrid in 1620, he thanked all of those allies by dedicating individual plays to them. Thus *Los locos de Valencia* (*Madness in Valencia*) first appears with a prologue dedicated to the humanist Simon Xabelo in which Lope defends his drama against the envy of his detractors and preens his own humanist feathers in public. In an overtly ostentatious display of erudition, Aristotle, Diogenes, and Plato are just three of the authorities cited to support his arguments.

Although the relationship between the play, Simon Xabelo and this bitterly vivid literary polemic may have been tenuously accidental, if not entirely incidental, it does point to the indistinct and flexible boundary which separated the tangible circumstances of Lope's life from his intangible artistic creations. Lope himself was aware of the (con)fusion of fact and fiction in his work and in a sonnet of *Rimas* addressed to Lupercio Leonardo de Argensola, he refers explicitly to his inability to keep his own love affairs out of his poetry. An ardent, if inconstant, lover, his wives and mistresses wander through the pages and stages of his prolific outpourings. The disguises are deliberately transparent. His first wife Isabel de Urbina is Belisa, his mistress Micaela de Luján is sometimes Celia, sometimes Camila Lucinda, while Marta de Nevares is Amarilis or Marcia Leonarda. But it is an early affair with the married actress Elena Osorio, who makes her début as Filis in the early sonnets of *Rimas* and takes her final curtain call in the autobiographical *La Dorotea* (1632), which has the most lasting impact on Lope's amorous imagination.

In fact we could say that Lope's artistic association with Valencia was a direct result of his failed affair with Elena. Frustrated by her rejection of him, Lope had exorcised his bitterness using the most powerful weapon at his disposal, his pen. His scathing attacks on her personal and professional life, implicating almost everyone involved in both, led to imprisonment and an enforced exile of four years from Madrid, at least two of these to be spent outside Castile. Lope, not surprisingly, observed only the spirit of this law. He failed to respect the conditions of his sentence by returning to Madrid to "collect" the wife (Isabel), whom he had previously abandoned there when he set off to sail the high seas. He did, however, spend two years in exile in Valencia (1588-1590). It was to be the first of three visits. The second was in 1599 on the occasion of the Royal Wedding of Philip III to Margaret of Austria, and the third and final visit occurred in 1616 when, as a fifty-four year-old priest, he left Madrid in pursuit of the actress Lucía Salcedo. Needless to say, whatever the varying circumstances which necessitated his trips to Valencia, the genuine affection which he felt for the city and its inhabitants emerges clearly from his work. He pays homage to Valencia in descriptive poems such as *Las fiestas de Denia*, in the prose work *El peregrino en su patria*, and of course in his drama: among others *El bobo del Colegio (The Fool in School)*, *Don Lope de Cardona*, *El prado de Valencia (A Valencian Field)*, *La viuda valenciana (The Widow of Valencia)*, and, naturally of most interest to us here, in *Los locos de Valencia*. Even a play unconcerned with Valencia, *Los españoles en Flandes (Spaniards in Flanders)*, is dedicated to one of its citizens, Cristóbal Ferreira de Sampayo, and is yet another pretext to eulogise the place and its people.

Paradoxically, perhaps, his explicit and genuine affection for the geographical setting of a play such as *Madness in Valencia* has been a distracting and deceptive influence in terms of the work's critical reception. The work has generally been relegated to the lower divisions of Lope's theatre. A promising, if immature, piece, it is usually discussed, if at all, as a complicated testing-ground for the complex expression of amorous intrigue and feigned madness, and of course, as a by-product of the circumstances of his exile. Indeed there is a supreme irony in the fact that the Valencian setting, and more specifically, the madhouse in which the main action of the play takes place, is foregrounded by commentators as a marvellously *real* backdrop against which the drama unfolds. The paradox of the asylum as a point of identification for Lope's seventeenth-century audience, indeed as their most concrete touchstone with reality, is largely overlooked.

As we can see from the accuracy of the references to it in the play, Lope was obviously familiar with the internal organisation of Spain's first and most famous mental hospital, proudly, though hyperbolically, describing it as "one of the seven wonders of the world". No doubt the methods employed by the administrators might seem rather barbaric to us now, but if we look beyond the austerity of the uniforms and cages, beyond the severity of the treatments et cetera, we can see that the approach taken was a radical step forward in mental healthcare. Unlike similar establishments of the time, the Valencian hospital was not concerned with the social alienation or marginalisation of the mad, but its ultimate objective was to cure them with a view to social reintegration. Lope's 'elastic' use of the dramatic space of the mental hospital, however, stretches far beyond a desire to demonstrate medical advances. It is in fact the most appropriate setting in which to dramatise the dramatic. For if it is true that certain texts require certain critical approaches to bring out their latent potential, then it may be equally true to say that the confusions at the heart of *Madness in Valencia*, both at the level of plot and of role identification, can only be fully illuminated in a metatheatrical light. It is not just that Lope's play has, until recently, been a victim of the linkage between canonicity and critical attention, but that the scant attention which it has received has confined it to the rigid boundaries of its own time.

An argument for universality of message and appeal does not, of course, negate an interpretation of the play as a work representative of the social and artistic concerns of its age. A seventeenth-century audience, for instance, would have been conditioned both by literary and medical texts not simply to accept the association of love and madness on stage, but, indeed, to expect it. Burton's contemporaneous *Anatomy of Melancholy* (1612) reveals that even long before Catullus felt a ringing in his ears at the sight of Lesbia, the melancholy of love, or malady of *hereos*, had been categorised in antiquity as a mental imbalance with varying degrees of physical and emotional symptoms. Indeed, in the Modern period, from the Middle Ages right through the Renaissance, there is a remarkable similarity in the depiction of *melancholia*, regardless of whether these descriptions have a scientific, philosophical or literary focus. The dominant explanation for lovesickness was invariably the malfunctioning of physical organs and usually, though sometimes not explicitly, the writers concerned invoked the humours theory proffered by the second century physician Galen. This is the case in Andreas Capellanus' amorous handbook *De amore*, the medical treatise of the Catalan doctor Arnaldus de Vilanova, the philosophical investigations of the sixteenth-century Spaniards Andrés Velázquez and Huarte de San Juan, among others, and the sentimental romances of Diego de San Pedro.

According to this theory, mental disorder emerged from an imbalance of the bodily fluids or humours. It was generally agreed that an excess of black bile was responsible for causing melancholia, but there were various opinions as to what caused the excess of bile in the first place. The influence of the planets on human temperaments was often cited as a convenient irremediable scapegoat. Renaissance Neoplatonists (such as Pico de la Mirandola) did their best to salvage the dismal reputation of the melancholic temperament, by emphasising its predisposition to the intellectual pursuits of poetry and philosophy, but they could not eradicate the popular belief that melancholics were the doomed disciples of Saturn, the most malign of the planets. (It is, of course, the temper of this very belief which was so vividly captured in Goya's gruesome nineteenth-century image of infanticide.) However, there were more immediate and curable causes of melancholy other than planetary destiny. It might be the result of eating "melancholic" food, the consumption of strong wines, or the consequence of excessive study or reading (as in the case of Don Quijote), even of anxiety, sadness or any number of psychological traumas, including, naturally, as in the case of Lope's Fedra, the rejection and frustration of unrequited love.

According to the logic of Renaissance thought, the frenzy associated with lovesickness might be quelled only if the guilty humour could be brought under control. Delirium could not be evaluated in psychological terms, and therefore had to be understood in terms of physiology. The medical philosophy of the Renaissance, characterised by a belief in the power of medicine to cure all the ills of man, can only be understood by the modern mind in the double context of the limitations of traditional medicine at the time, and of the persistence of the Medieval understanding of a God-centred universe. The divine organisation of the universe meant that the natural world had all the resources necessary to counterbalance the disorders of the human body, and it was the Christian doctor's duty to uncover these mysterious curative substances. The theory of humoral medicine underlined, therefore, the relation of microcosm to macrocosm, and confirmed the human being's place in the great chain of being and the epistemological order of things. There was, of course, as Michel Foucault has argued, an evolving reorganisation of the structure of thought in sixteenth and seventeenth-century Europe, which threatened to replace the system of analogical thinking, operative from ancient times, with a system based on logical identity and difference. Philosophical, mathematical and scientific discoveries pointed to a new understanding of the world in which the emphasis was placed on human autonomy, exemplified by the Cartesium dictum *Cogito, ergo sum.*

The older system, however, as most commentators of Spanish Golden Age drama recognise, lends itself more readily to literary images and representation. Hence the continued recourse in Renaissance literature to Medieval theories, such as that of humoral medicine. On the other hand, the insistence on a theocentric understanding of the universe might well have been a response to those who would challenge traditional thinking and supplant divine ordinance with human authority. We could argue that Lope de Vega's exploitation of lovesickness in this play, and others, goes beyond a desire to emulate elegist and Petrarchan literary precedents, and is, in fact, a reaffirmation of the harmonious structuring of his world and the existence of a greater world beyond.

Indeed Lope's exploitation of the *mundo al revés topos* (that of the world upside-down) in *Madness in Valencia* might also be considered in a similar vein. It is a dramatic motif with an impressive pedigree. Its origins can be traced back to Antilochus, to Virgilian *adynata*, to the *disparates* of Juan del Encina, and to the numerous engravings (or *aleluyas*: see Lorca's *The Love of Don Perlimplin*) which depict men and women standing on their heads, maps with countries in reverse position, flying fish and swimming birds and, just as ridiculous for observers of the period, human beings involved in situations of role reversal. In a Christian context the world was turned upside-down by the Fall of Lucifer and the disobedience of Adam and Eve. Consequently, changes in the existing order were viewed as dangerous, and the work of the devil as the result of man's folly or of sinfulnesss. In post-Tridentine seventeenth-century Spain the theme was a prevalent one and a particularly appropriate reflection of *desengaño* (disillusionment) with the world. Whether or not the aim was sociopolitically subversive is difficult to judge for certain, and different authors would have worked to their own particular agenda, but the comic spirit which characterised it is incontrovertible. In theatre this *enseñar deleitando* (to teach through entertainment) aspect of the play was often rooted in a desire to reassure the audience that it did know when the world was the right way up and that things could be restored to order after they had been turned upside-down.

Order, then, as a seventeenth-century audience would have understood it, is confused, but ultimately reassuringly restored in Lope's *Los locos de Valencia*. Social boundaries, flouted by feigned madness, are re-established as, in accordance with comic convention, the customary marriages close out the action. This is not the case, however, in David Johnston's adaptation for performance, *Madness in Valencia*. Laida, the servant, is not conveniently paired off in the final scene to her social equal, Leonato, who in the original version returns as the Gentleman's manservant in Act 3, Scene 8. That would be impossible; mainly because Leonato exits Johnston's version after he unceremoniously dumps Erifila in the third scene of Act I. Why the change? Well, Leonato's return serves a double function at the end of Lope's drama. He is not simply needed as a partner for Laida. He is also required to expose the true identity of Erifilia and to testify to her sanity, and to her virginity. She is therefore "pure" enough to marry Floriano. (His innocence is confirmed in turn by the "resurrection" of Reinero. He did not commit the terrible crime of killing above his station after all, the victim was a mere servant, and Floriano, pronounced "sane" can now marry his beloved.) Leonato's return, however, poses other complications for Lope, who must explain away his morally dubious action earlier on in the drama as a reaction to fear of Erifila's irate father. Of course he still has her money and jewels which he can now return to her and be exonerated. Valerio too does the decent thing and marries Fedra. Fortunately, neither has really transgressed in the course of the action, though not for want of trying. The fact that they had never given one another a second glance before now is irrelevant. Comedy demands the "feel good" factor and, we imagine, they all live happily ever after.

However much the literary critic's sensibilities may be offended by what can still be considered Lope's "caving in" to social and generic convention, despite the argument for a reaffirmation of the epistemological order, a post-Cartesian contemporary audience would find the social conveniences of the dénouement particularly hard to swallow. So Johnston offers them their moment of pathos. Leonato does not return at the end and Laida is left frustrated and alone on stage looking for lost pebbles. It is, though, only a momentary concession. Johnston has gone to great lengths to produce a version of this play which respects the integrity of the comic spirit of the original. This, as any linguist will confirm, is no easy task. Humour is not a flexible cross-cultural commodity. The details of it do not transfer easily from one language to another. Nor does it travel well through time. The playful set-piece images of Lope, often judged the artistic embodiment of the *homo ludens,* could be easily absorbed in a modern version. The flexible farcicalities of the plot could, for the most part, be "faithfully" represented. But what can a translator do when the humour resides in remote concepts or allusions, no longer funny or non-identifiable to a modern audience? Or worse still, perhaps, when the serious elements of the original have a modern audience rolling in the aisles at inappropriate moments? The answer is obvious, but unfortunately, not yet redundant. The play must be made to work on stage. If this involves updating concepts and modernising allusions, or even making "straight" characters funny, the translator can make no apology for that.

On his reinvention of Lope's Doctor, David Johnston has said: "It was clearly not possible to recreate this functional role [...] so I decided to highlight the Doctor's more comic elements, enlivening his interaction with other characters in the asylum by turning his long disquisitions on the nature and tell-tale signs of sanity and madness into hopelessly inadequate, essentially comic, personality tests based on the association of ideas [...] Not that I felt guilty about this, because I remained convinced that those scenes of the play involving the Doctor could not

17

have worked without such a change. And the change itself was hardly radical after all, because what I had done was to hook this character onto one of the main thematic axes of the work – the relativity of madness and sanity." (*Stages of Translation*, Absolute Classics, 1997, p. 6) This was his response to a radio programme in which two critics, who had seen his version of Lope's play in performance, failed to see that it was just that, a version, and now believed Lope to be an "unsuspected precursor of Freud". The idea that two distinct voices, that of original author and translator, could sing a perfectly harmonious duet, without always following the same line of music, was evidently beyond them.

Lovesickness, then, in this version, is not and could not be taken seriously. But there is a metadramatic message at the heart of Lope's play as pertinent today as in seventeenth-century Spain, and in *Madness in Valencia* David Johnston recreates Lope de Vega's multi-level theatrical experience for the modern-day audience. All the original metatheatrical devices are intact (role-playing, the ceremony within the play, the use of real life and literary references, et cetera) and underpinning it all is the notion of madness as a performable state. The emphasis is on the theatricality of madness as a condition which displays itself in gait, demeanour, habits, costume, and of course, speech. For in this play it is the linguistic freedom of madness which makes it the great social and artistic leveller. It is at once a protective, inebriating, contagious force propelling the action in ever-spiralling circles of confusing delusion. For it is *all* delusion. This madness itself is feigned, and the idea of sanity cloaked in madness serves to highlight how the boundaries between the two can be so easily blurred. Even the language which expresses this lunacy is deceptive. For what it expresses is the calculated performance of the sane, and therefore it is not a private system of incoherencies, or meanings inaccessible to the rational world of the audience. It is a self-conscious eloquence which constantly breaks mimetic reality and produces the conflict between illusion and reality. In *Madness in Valencia* the stock phrases of Baroque Spain are confirmed: all the world *is* a stage and life *is* a dream.

Just as Lope exploited the intertextual experience of his audience, David Johnston flashes through the mind's eye of an

English-speaking contemporary audience distorted images of, at the very least, his top ten of greatest literary hits. Like his Doctor Verino he comically exploits allusive reference and association of ideas. Recruiting the help of Ecclesiastes, Shakespeare, Wilfred Owen, Robbie Burns, W B Yeats and Cervantes, among others, he manages to transfer Lope de Vega's relentless humour and energy successfully to the modern stage. At the end of the day this is a very funny play and misguided attempts to overemphasise its profundities would only serve to decomicalise it. A churlish audience might find Reinero's final speech, which condemns the entire play as unnecessary, somewhat annoying. But then not seeing the funny side of life might be the maddest act of all. At least, I imagine that's what Lope would probably say.

Isabel Torres
Queen's University, Belfast, July 1997

Characters

FLORIANO

VALERIO

ERIFILA

LEONATO

PISANO

MARTIN

THOMAS

FEDRA

LAIDA

LIBERTO

SANCHO

VERINO

BELARDO, a madman

MORDACHO, a madman

MADMEN

MADNESS IN VALENCIA was first performed at the
Gate Theatre on the 15th December 1992 by the following
ensemble of actors:

Sasha Behar, Christian Flint, Sean French, Simon Kunz,
Caroline Long, Sarah Malin, John Straiton, Mark Sproston,
Martin Turner, Nik Zeps

Director: Laurence Boswell

Assistant Director: Gaynor MacFarlane

Designer: Rae Smith

ACT ONE

Scene 1

A wood on the outskirts of Valencia, beside the city's famous mad-house.

FLORIANO: Valerio, I'm over here.

VALERIO: I came as quickly as I could,
   as soon as your message arrived.

FLORIANO: It took me four days to get here,
   riding hard from Zaragoza,
   with the devil himself behind me.

VALERIO: Your face is the colour of death.

FLORIANO: There was no one else I could trust...
   you're the only friend I've got left.

VALERIO: Tell me for God's sake what you've done.

FLORIANO: I...

VALERIO: What?

FLORIANO: I...

VALERIO: You what?

FLORIANO: I... ah... killed...

VALERIO: Holy God in heaven! Murdered?
   You mean you've murdered someone? Who?

FLORIANO: A man... are you sure we're alone?

VALERIO: Positive. Tell me, who was it?

FLORIANO: A man who'd've destroyed me if...

VALERIO: Floriano, stand still, will you,
   there's not a soul for miles around,
   except the crazed creatures in there.

23

FLORIANO: Try and put yourself in my place,
    every rustle, every murmur...

VALERIO: Calm down and tell me who it was.

FLORIANO: They'll be scouring the whole country,
    I can't even trust my own shadow.

VALERIO: You're in a worse state than your victim...
    you're a mess of nerves.

FLORIANO: I panicked.
    I stole a horse and we bolted
    from Zaragoza to Valencia,
    down lonely country tracks and lanes,
    begging bread from the odd goatherd,
    though I've been hungry for four days.
    That's what happened. In a nutshell.

VALERIO: Let's see if we can crack the nut.
    Who was it?

FLORIANO: If I'm seen, I'm dead.

VALERIO: Some gentleman? No... not a priest?

FLORIANO: In God's name, I swear I don't know.

VALERIO: Then, my friend, you are dead indeed,
    for if you refuse to trust me
    and keep on playing foolish games...

FLORIANO: All right, I'll tell you who it was...
    He was a nobleman... a prince,
    a sort of prince.

VALERIO: What sort of prince?

FLORIANO: Prince Reinero...

VALERIO: Reinero! He's...

FLORIANO: I know... tenth in line to the throne.
    I've had four days to work it out.

VALERIO: They'll hunt you to the ends of the earth,
    like hounds close down a fox.

FLORIANO: Thank you.
    I knew I could rely on you.

VALERIO: God knows, if I could give my life
    for yours, then you'd be a free man.
    If I could bring him back to life
    with the love that I have for you...
    but your sin is against God and man.
    Though danger can sharpen the wits
    and invention may save you yet.
    We must think. (*Silence.*) How did it happen?
    How did you get past all those guards?

FLORIANO: Let's get one thing clear – I killed him.
    I did not assassinate him!
    It was bad luck, sheer misfortune
    that brought him and me face to face
    in the house of a certain lady...
    Celia... she's got the loveliest eyes...

VALERIO: More blood's been spilt for the sake of love
    than in all man's battles and wars.

FLORIANO: Believe me, I'd no taste for blood...
    I just wanted to get away,
    but he flew into a fury
    and would listen to no reason.
    There were two guards waiting outside
    and he set them on me like dogs.
    I ran into a narrow lane
    and he came thundering after me.
    I knew that I was about to die
    and with the courage of the dead
    I drew my sword and turned round.
    His guards had no room to get past,
    and I ran my sword through his arm,
    and plunged it clean into his heart.
    He fell like an ox at slaughter.

VALERIO: You're absolutely sure he's dead?

FLORIANO: I drove my sword in to the hilt
 and felt his blood run down my wrist.
 Then I turned on my heels and ran,
 thanking God for my good fortune,
 for to stay would have tempted fate,
 and I heard a voice crying out:
 'You'll not escape us, you bastard;
 this is no ordinary man you've killed,
 but Reinero, a grandee of Spain.'
 My blood froze, though thank God not my feet,
 and long before the cold dawn broke
 I'd put ten miles between them and me.
 Fear can be the cruellest, sharpest spur.

VALERIO: There's no telling where they might be,
 they could be as far north as France
 or as far south as hot Seville.

FLORIANO: Or waiting round the next corner.

VALERIO: There's nowhere in Spain you are safe,
 and there is no easy escape.
 Your sword is bigger than your brain.
 God damn your recklessness in love!
 I'm being pulled in all directions...
 a thousand possibilities
 and not a hope that's hard and fast.
 How can I keep a king at bay?
 How could I hope to shelter you
 in a town full of prying eyes?
 There's nowhere you won't create a stir.
 Unless... unless... the asylum!
 Could you pretend to have gone mad,
 you know, ranting, raving, so on,
 so that they take you for a loony?

FLORIANO: Do you think I'm not already?
 But I'll not have any madhouse,
 I've seen the wretches they torture there.

VALERIO: There's an asylum in Valencia
    as famous as the world is wide,
    where all sorts of fits and frenzies
    are treated and cured with science.
    If you go into the madhouse
    your enemies will think you dead.

FLORIANO: In rags, in dirt, amongst the mad...

VALERIO: I think you may well benefit,
    and besides, it's your only hope.

FLORIANO: Valerio, you've saved my life!
    I'll rant and rave to such effect,
    even you will doubt my sanity.

VALERIO: Just act as though you were in love.
    What greater madness is there?

Scene 2

Enter ERIFILA and LEONATO, both dressed in travelling clothes.

LEONATO: Thank God, Valencia at last,
    the city of love and war.
    You can see the walls over there,
    and the banks of the Turia
    as it flows down towards the sea.
    Perhaps we can find some peace here,
    a bed to lie down together.

ERIFILA: Everywhere looks so green and lush.

LEONATO: They call this the orchard of Spain,
    a place for our love to grow green.

FLORIANO: Do you know them?

VALERIO: No, they're strangers.
    Let's go.

FLORIANO: God, you don't think that they're...

VALERIO: They're a pair of lovers, that's all,
    as mad as you in their own way.
    Let's get you to the asylum.
    I know the administrator.
    He has a house within the grounds.

Scene 3

ERIFILA: This is a paradise.

LEONATO: Maybe.

ERIFILA: I feel so free, so fortunate,
    so far away from my father.
    Do you think he'll come after us?

LEONATO: He'll wash his hands of us for ever,
    and do what all gentlefolk do.
    Try to silence the wagging tongues,
    say you're no longer his daughter
    and that his servant betrayed him.

ERIFILA: If he knew how much I loved you,
    then he would say that I was crazed.

LEONATO reacts angrily to this final word.

LEONATO: Then perhaps it is a madness.
    You and I lived in different worlds.
    I beg you, choose your words with care,
    for the love that I have for you
    makes me equal to any man.
    I'm not longer just your servant.

ERIFILA: I've never thought of you like that!

LEONATO: Careless words betray a doubting heart.

ERIFILA: Tell me, what have my words betrayed?

LEONATO: Your every word, your silences,
    speak eloquently of regret.

ERIFILA: I've given you my soul, my life,
the two dearest things I possess,
I gave them willingly to you.
How can you take offence from that,
and how can you talk of madness?

LEONATO: It was you spoke of being crazed.
The servant and his master's daughter.
That's not love... it's a laughing stock.

ERIFILA: Have you suddenly become less?
I fell in love with a servant
because you were my father's servant.
But my eyes saw you as you were
and I love you now as you are.

LEONATO: What could you see? Contempt, disdain...
all these things are invisible.
But I lived them, day in, day out.
Contempt, disdain, in every look,
in every word that's been uttered.

ERIFILA: You're the one who's crazy.

LEONATO: Crazy?
Because I stand up for myself?

ERIFILA: Stand up for yourself against what?
What imaginary offence?
That it was madness to run away?
That I was crazed with love for you?

LEONATO: I can hear what's behind those words
and I can see what's in your heart.

ERIFILA: Who better to read it than you?
It is yours through love and reason.
But if all you seek is an excuse
to leave me here alone, then go.

LEONATO: You pour insult upon insult.
You call your love 'a mere madness'

and you think me a man of no shame
who'd abandon you in this wood.
I said choose your words with great care.

ERIFILA: I don't know you, Leonato.
Dark thoughts have taken hold of you
and blinded you to who I am.

LEONATO: Disdain for disdain, my lady.
I've come to my senses at last.

ERIFILA: Did I ever say you'd lost them?

LEONATO: Yes.

ERIFILA: No, I didn't!

LEONATO: Yes, you did!

ERIFILA: Take that back, because it's not true.

LEONATO: What's a servant but a liar.
If you had loved me, as you claim,
you would have slept and lain with me,
not whined on about your honour,
about what you call your honour.
And my tears and pleas fell like seed
on the hard ground of your dead heart.
You say you saw me and loved me?
You've never looked at anyone
in your life; your eyes are as blind
as your heart is cold.

ERIFILA: My honour
is as precious to me as life,
and until you are my husband
it remains mine and mine alone.
I've given you no excuses
and I'll accept no reproaches.
What if I had lain down with you?
Where would you have been the next day?

Like all men, your pleas come easy,
easy come just as easy go.

LEONATO: Desire pays no heed to honour
and the fire that burns before
is only fanned all the more by love;
your excuse? You didn't trust me.
A fiction, a fantasy, a lie.
There's not a single word you've said
that's not been rotten through and through.
Tell me I'm wrong, that you love me,
that your airs and graces, your contempt,
are a figment of my dark thoughts.

ERIFILA: You're a fool.

LEONATO: I've been made a fool.

ERIFILA: If I'd taken you for a fool,
if my love were as false as you say,
would I have left my parents' house,
left my city, risked everything?

LEONATO: It was hatred not love brought you here.
Hatred for your parents, for your home,
not love for a simple servant.

ERIFILA: Hatred? Why? I hated no one.
Was life at home so hard for me,
and my own beauty so lacking
that I had to seek a match in you?
I could've married a thousand times.
My parents would have wept for joy.
But I chose you. We've said harsh words.
They will make our love grow stronger
if we can force them from our minds.

LEONATO: Then let us force them from our minds.
(*Silence.*) Where are the jewels?

ERIFILA: What jewels?

31

LEONATO: The ones that you had in your bag.
I need them to pay for an inn.

ERIFILA: You mean that we've no money left?

LEONATO: Not a peseta.

ERIFILA: Sell this then.

LEONATO: I want them all.

ERIFILA: All of them?

LEONATO: Now.

ERIFILA: How do I know that you'll come back?

LEONATO: You'll pay for that insult, my lady.

ERIFILA: I'm not your lady, I love you!
You don't have to steal my jewels.
They belong to you already,
like everything else that is mine.
You are my husband.

LEONATO: No I'm not!
Give me the jewels, lying bitch.

ERIFILA: Why are you doing this to me?

LEONATO: Give them to me or I'll kill you.

He unsheaths a dagger.

ERIFILA: You're showing your true colours now.

LEONATO: All of them!

ERIFILA: There aren't any more.
Put it away.

LEONATO: It's gone.
(*He sheaths the dagger.*) Your cloak.

ERIFILA: My cloak, what for?

LEONATO: Stay calm.

ERIFILA: Stay calm!

LEONATO: Another word and I'll kill you.

ERIFILA: You'd kill me for speaking? You are mad!

He unsheaths the dagger.

LEONATO: Your cloak.

ERIFILA: Don't hurt me.

LEONATO: Then don't speak.
(*He sheaths the dagger.*) Now take off the rest of your
clothes.

ERIFILA: My clothes?

LEONATO: Take them off.

ERIFILA: No, please don't...

LEONATO: By Christ, I said another word
and I'd cut you from arse to tit!

He unsheaths the dagger.

ERIFILA: I feel sick!

LEONATO: Stop pretending!

ERIFILA: Please!

He looks at her with contempt.

LEONATO: I wouldn't waste my strength on you.
What's it like to have nothing?
What's it like to feel ashamed?

He makes to leave.

ERIFILA: You can't leave me here like this?

LEONATO: No?

ERIFILA: Then kill me, I don't give a damn.

LEONATO: That would be too easy for you.

ERIFILA: Bastard! Bastard! Wait for me... please.

LEONATO: What is there for me to wait for?

LEONATO disappears, leaving ERIFILA standing naked in the clearing.

Scene 4

ERIFILA: What else could I have expected?
He's gone, left me here high and dry.
What in God's name am I to do now,
alone in a strange country
with no money and no name,
not even a shirt for my back?
Treacherous coward! Brute! Pig!
God knows, he was always a coward.
A servant with a servant's soul.
But he was a cunning bastard
and I really thought I had him fooled,
that I was besotted with him,
that I couldn't wait another day
before leaving my loving parents
with him. He was right. Who was he?
The vile servant of a hard father
who wanted his daughter married,
who talked and thought of nothing else.
I'm a thousand times better off
here than there, married to my cousin.
At least he took only my clothes.
How can I go anywhere like this?
I told him I was mad for him,
that I could think of nothing else;
for years I've thought of my escape,
for years I thought of nothing else,
and now I can't think for myself.
If I stay here, I'll go insane.

She hears voices and hides.

Scene 5

Enter VALERIO, PISANO, MARTIN and THOMAS. ERIFILA has hidden.

PISANO: He's certainly in a bad way;
    ranting and raving, furious,
    snarling at his own shadow,
    reciting speeches from Shakespeare
    and spewing white foam from his mouth
    like a hungry dog in a butcher's.

VALERIO: He couldn't be in better hands.

PISANO: You've seen the administrator?
    He'll have told you how advanced
    Valencian medicine is
    when it comes to treating loonies.

VALERIO: I'm not sure about medicines.
    Perhaps we should just wait and see.

PISANO: Personally, I'd have him locked up.
    We keep twenty wooden cages
    with cleaner straw than any inn.
    That's where we put the wilder ones.
    For their own good, you understand.

VALERIO: He'll calm down when the full moon wanes.
    If he finds himself locked away
    he'll fall into melancholy
    and be dead before the night's out.
    Let him move freely with the rest
    of the poor innocents that live here.

PISANO: You'll assume responsibility?

VALERIO: Fully.

PISANO: Name?

VALERIO: Orlando.

PISANO: That's it?

VALERIO: His family name is... Furioso.

PISANO: Orlando Furioso...
   That has a familiar ring.
   Where's he from?

VALERIO: From Italy.
   A dangerously hot-blooded race.

PISANO: Well he was ranting in Spanish.

VALERIO: Remarkable. The gift of tongues.
   His mother was Spanish, I think.

ERIFILA: (*Aside.*) If they see me like this, I'm lost.
   They'll have me in a cage with him.

PISANO: His profession?

VALERIO: Scholar and critic.

PISANO: Of philosophy?

VALERIO: Of plays.

PISANO: Ah!
   I've known other cases like his.

VALERIO: There's an added complication.
   Love.

PISANO: A sorry combination.
   Actors tend to addle the brains
   while Cupid enrages the heart.

VALERIO: It's no wonder wise men counsel
   that we treat love and books like the plague.

PISANO: In all things, great moderation.

Here we study the roots of madness:
the lack of food that starves the brain,
the moon that crazes human reason,
excessive devotion to books,
the blind pursuit of the passions
(of which love and masturbation
are the most dangerous by far).
Look at these two for example.

VALERIO: What about them?

PISANO: They were scholars
who wrote all sorts of treatises
and learned works on things obscure:
philosophy, astronomy,
and dreams of impossible things.
They teetered on the edge of sanity
for years in their university...
Then one day they both fell in love...

VALERIO: With each other?

PISANO: With the same girl.
Two weeks later they were in here.
We had them locked up for a year,
to calm their blood. Now they work well.
We even let them go into town
to beg for alms. Thomas, come here.

ERIFILA: (*Aside.*) How can I get away from here?

PISANO: (*Patting THOMAS on the head.*) Well, son, what have
                                     you got to say?

THOMAS: I was my father's son all right.
He's dead and gone... who does that leave me?

PISANO: Martin, do you know who you are?

MARTIN: Yes, but I don't want him to hear...
He believes he's Don Quijote,
just a character in a book.

I should know... didn't I write it?

VALERIO: Martin thinks that he's Cervantes?

PISANO: Who?

MARTIN: There's a woman over there!

THOMAS: Sweet Dulcinea awaits me!

MARTIN: I wrote the book! That means she's mine.
    I'm going to make you a donkey!

ERIFILA: (*Aside.*) There's only one way out of this...
    (*She emerges clad in leaves.*) Help me, God in heaven!
    Justice!

MARTIN and THOMAS kneel.

THOMAS: Dulcinea!

MARTIN: Sweet forest nymph!
    Do you fancy a part in a book?

ERIFILA: Oh kind sirs, help me, I beg you.
    A poor maiden in deep distress
    who has been robbed of her jewels
    and her clothes and left here for dead.

PISANO: Then we have arrived just in time.

VALERIO: I swear I took her for an inmate.

ERIFILA: Scarcely had I come to this fair place
    when a highwayman, a bandit
    set about me.

THOMAS: My poor lady!

ERIFILA: What?

THOMAS: Stand still I beg you.

ERIFILA: What for?

THOMAS: So that I may do you homage.
　My knightly pursuits demand it.

ERIFILA: I had enough nightly pursuits
　from Leonato. Get off me!

PISANO: No, she's not an inmate of ours
　though I'm quite sure she soon will be.
　Such intemperance!

ERIFILA:　　　　　Can you blame me?
　(*To VALERIO.*) Kind sir, you are a gentleman,
　and can see the distress I am in.
　Everything I had has been taken.

MARTIN: Even her brainpan's been ransacked.

ERIFILA: My jewels were worth a fortune,
　a king's ransom in emeralds.

PISANO: That's it: that's the locus dementis.
　'Every wiseman hath his problem,
　every madman his obsession.'
　It holds true of madwomen too.

THOMAS: Who's Leonato? Your lover?

ERIFILA: I'd kill any man said he was.

THOMAS: Harsh words spoken to your sworn knight,
　one who lives and breathes for his lady.

PISANO: Thomas!

MARTIN:　　　　Does she know who you are?

ERIFILA: He doesn't even know who he is!

MARTIN: I'll have her after.

ERIFILA:　　　　　　　You'll do what?
　If you were knights or gentlemen,
　one of you would give me a cape
　so that I may cover myself

39

and be on my way.

PISANO: She's cunning.
At times she seems to reason well,
but the source of her madness is clear.
Grab her!

ERIFILA: Grab me? What have I done?

PISANO: Go on, grab her!

ERIFILA: You try it, knight,
and you'll never right another wrong.

THOMAS: Moorish whore! Prison for you!

ERIFILA: Prison? Why prison in God's name?
What have I done to merit this abuse?
There's not a drop of common sense
among the whole damned crew of you.

PISANO: Take an arm each.

ERIFILA: I came for help,
I told you that I had been robbed...
Is this your idea of justice?
What sort of place is Valencia?

PISANO: You'll come to thank us for this act.
Your tortured mind's oblivious
to the concern we feel for you.

ERIFILA: So why are you kidnapping me
and taking me to a madhouse?
I was robbed! My jewels and my clothes!

PISANO: (*To VALERIO.*) The locus dementis... never fails.
(*Loudly.*) You must tell that to the doctor.

ERIFILA: Would it not make a lot more sense
to arrest the robber and not the robbed?

PISANO: This obsession clearly runs deep.

40

MARTIN: Giddy up.

ERIFILA: Get your hands off me!
    Robbed and imprisoned in one day!
    I can't believe this.

The two madmen lead her away.

PISANO: I must go.
    We can meet again tomorrow.

VALERIO: Please thank the administrator
    on my behalf for his kindness.
    Orlando will be much better
    if he's not locked away to rot.
    He's not a violent man at all
    and his fury will soon subside.

ERIFILA: (*Shouting, off.*) Try that once more and I'll split
                                            your head!

VALERIO: Compared to that demented creature...

PISANO: I haven't met a loony yet
    who isn't violent at full moon.
    And we've discovered something else,
    through scientific observation;

MARTIN cries out in pain, off.

    they all have the strength of ten men.

VALERIO: Fascinating.

PISANO: The first sign and...

VALERIO: Then you must do as you see fit.

Exit PISANO.

Scene 6

VALERIO: Fortune's made me its fool today
   and brought me to the gates of death.
   Filled with fear, I took Floriano
   into the very pit of hell,
   a sane man into the madhouse.
   But it's the madman who comes out.
   When I saw her, that strange woman,
   I felt my senses drain and fill.
   I don't know if I've lost my mind
   or even if I've one left to lose.
   I've never seen such perfection;
   she wounded my eyes, then my heart,
   and I could do nothing but stare,
   not knowing if she was an angel
   or a woman of flesh and blood.
   And I let them take her away.
   The fool stood in simple silence
   when he should have defended her,
   offered her help, refuge, a home.
   I am a witless oaf, a coward,
   for my soul tells me she is sane,
   for if she's not, I'm the madman.
   The lover mirrors the beloved,
   that much is clear to all who love.
   I have to see her again to test
   the evidence of my senses.
   But if I return to that place,
   then they'll have me in their cages
   to cleanse this madness from my soul.

Scene 7

The asylum yard. FEDRA and LAIDA appear.

FEDRA: Tell me, just what's so important
   that it couldn't wait till later?

Dragging me down to this cold yard,
with all the loonies watching us.

LAIDA: It's not my fault... it's a madness
within my soul... a joy... a rage.
Now the administrator's gone out...

FEDRA: What's my uncle to do with this?

LAIDA: He's been a good master to me
but if he knew I was in love...
I brought you down here to see him.

FEDRA: No, Laida... it's not one of them?
A loony? Madness is contagious.

LAIDA: Love knows no measure or restraint,
otherwise it would not be love.

FEDRA: And you feel love for a madman?

LAIDA: Love sees beyond the sight of eyes.

FEDRA: He's sucked your brains dry already.
If you had brains in the first place,
which I doubt.

LAIDA: He seemed sane to me;
it wasn't anything he said.
He stood there in total silence,
and in that silence touched my heart.

FEDRA: How can silence move you to love?

LAIDA: Any beautiful object can...
a lovely painting or a book.
He was as lovely as marble.

FEDRA: Then there's no hope for you, Laida.
You're in love with a raving fool.

LAIDA: I told you, Fedra, he doesn't rave;
he just stood in silence and stared.

FEDRA: Because he thinks he's made of stone.

LAIDA: The most beautiful stone, Fedra.

FEDRA: I feel sorry for you.

LAIDA: Don't be.

FEDRA: Does he fly into mad furies?

LAIDA: With the moon, and next full moon time
    I'll share in his fury with him,
    for my love grows like his fury
    under the sun of his beauty.

FEDRA: You're as mad as your marble statue,
    him and his moon, you and your sun.
    A fine pair. Where's your idiot from?

LAIDA: From Italy... mm... Italy.

FEDRA: I hope this statue speaks Spanish.

LAIDA: My lady, how little you know.
    Love has made me Italian too!
    (*She sings.*) La sensazione d'amore!

Scene 8

FLORIANO appears wearing a hospital tunic. He feigns violent madness.

FLORIANO: Chains! Chains! You talk to me of chains!
    I am a guest in this castle,
    a stranger in Valencia.
    Well, my false and deceitful host,
    do your worst, you'll not frighten me.
    So you've changed into a giant;
    an old trick, can't you do better?
    I could fell you with just one blow!

FEDRA: Sweet God, he's going to kill us all!

LAIDA: No, wait... something has upset him.
    His spirit is gentle and kind.

FEDRA: Laida... he's mad... crazy... insane.

FLORIANO: Good ladies, I wish you no harm;
    consider me at your service.
    Please don't be alarmed, stay here.
    I'm not the violent madman you think,
    no savage from wild America
    nor barbarian from the north.
    It was love brought me to this place,
    love that reduced me to this state.
    I am a man I cannot be
    and have simply fled from who I was.
    I have clothed myself in this madness.
    I was the most wretched of men,
    one who loved a noble lady,
    a creature of fire and snow
    who inspired love in all around.
    And in particular in one
    who came down to her from heaven,
    who turned her head with promises
    of glory and of power.
    And so I clipped this angel's wings.

FEDRA: Oh Laida!

LAIDA: Oh Fedra!

FLORIANO: He fell
    and I took flight and hid my face
    in this madness in Valencia.

FEDRA: Your story would cause stones to weep.

FLORIANO: I still walk in fear of my life;
    my heart pounds with every question;
    every day's a waking nightmare
    of gallows, of finding myself
    suddenly hanging in mid-air...

of the rack and burning irons.
I have poured out my heart to you,
and beg you to keep my secret.

LAIDA: You like him too... it's in your eyes.

FEDRA: Any woman would be the moon
    that inspires this man's madness.

LAIDA: So his madness has touched you too...

FEDRA: But how sane his words seemed to me...

LAIDA: Riddled with obsession and desire.

FEDRA: No, he spoke with passion, with force.

LAIDA: (*Pointedly.*) Yes, mistress.

FEDRA: I'm intrigued... that's all.

FLORIANO: When passion boils into jealousy
    then the mind is indeed at risk.
    But there are innumerable cures
    bequeathed to us by the ancients.
    Cool lavender oil on the brain
    so that its scent dulls the senses;
    then a series of slaps to the face.
    In more extreme cases, bat's blood
    has been favoured by the doctors
    and philosophers of Athens.
    But if the jealousy is horned,
    then there is no cure possible;
    even Pan on high Olympus,
    for all his pipes and magic ways,
    found his jealousy eternal.
    I too have lived in that abyss.
    I tell you: to love is to fear,
    to build castles of suspicion,
    towers of doubt, from no cause at all.

FEDRA: Does this sound like madness to you?

There is a terrible clarity
in everything he has to say.

FLORIANO: My lady, may I beg a token,
a requiescat in pace
for the man I was and have buried?

FEDRA: What can I give you?

FLORIANO: Your ribbon,
as a talisman to keep me sane,
a reminder of the bright sun
I saw today in this dark place.

FEDRA: And my ribbon will be all that?

FLORIANO: That it comes from you makes of it
a holy grail, my guiding star.

LAIDA: Such nobility of purpose
demands a purple ribbon.
Take mine... it happens to be purple.

FLORIANO: I ask for the holy grail
and you offer me a clay cup.

LAIDA: (*Aside.*) I was right to be on my guard.

FEDRA: Take this: the ribbon you need is green
for green's the colour of hope.

LAIDA: Remember what you said before,
about madness being contagious?

FEDRA: For heaven's sake, Laida, you fool,
I'm simply keeping him amused,
putting up with all his nonsense
just to keep him under control.
I've suffered a thousand deaths here.

LAIDA: Your propriety knows no bounds.

FLORIANO: (*Aside.*) Her beauty is a temptation,
and Celia, what are you for me
but a sour and bloody memory?
You betrayed me. I can betray you.

FEDRA: Sweet Jesus... there's someone coming.
They mustn't find me here like this!

LAIDA: Oh no, God forbid. Come with me.
You've your reputation to think of.

They leave.

FLORIANO: And now the warming sun has gone,
the darkness seems all the blacker.
Think of me, my lovely lady,
when you've nothing better to do.

Scene 9

Enter PISANO, THOMAS and MARTIN, dragging ERIFILA behind them.

ERIFILA: Why are you doing this to me?

PISANO: That's enough ranting and raving
or you'll find yourself in a cage.
You're as mad as a whore in Lent.

ERIFILA: I was once, I'll not deny it,
but not any more. One more thing.
I'm not a whore. Quite the reverse.

THOMAS: Here's the chapel. I'll keep vigil
over my arms and your honour,
my lady. But you must pay a toll.

ERIFILA: What?

MARTIN: Otherwise you don't get in.

ERIFILA: Fine by me.

PISANO: Then you go to jail.
  That's the law in Valencia.

ERIFILA: What am I supposed to pay with?
  Didn't I tell you I was robbed?

MARTIN: You either pay or go to jail.

PISANO: I wouldn't recommend the jail.
  They're not as gentle as we are.

FLORIANO: What's going on?

MARTIN: Stay out of this.

THOMAS: If you're a knight, tell me your name
  and your station.

ERIFILA: (*Aside.*)   I can't think straight,
  though that's little surprise in here.
  I could never survive in jail.
  There's only one choice: I'll be mad.

PISANO: I'll speak to the administrator.
  Stay here... and no funny business.

  Aside as he leaves.

  Some hope in here.

Scene 10

FLORIANO: (*Aside.*)   What loveliness!
  I've never seen such perfection;
  her face shines as bright as the sun,
  leaving darkness all around her
  and plunging me in confusion.

THOMAS: You can pay later.

MARTIN: She'll pay now.

FLORIANO: My very good friends! Er... colleagues.

MARTIN: Do you mean us?

FLORIANO: Indeed I do.
What is it that she has to pay?

THOMAS: Her entrance toll.

FLORIANO: I'll pay for her.
How much do you think this ring is worth?

MARTIN: Let me see it?

THOMAS: It's a beauty!

MARTIN: I suppose you'll want it back later,
when she's given us her money.

FLORIANO: You can sell it. And buy some food.

THOMAS: Sir, you are a knight among knights.

MARTIN: Tonight we'll have rabbit and wine,
and wine, and some rabbit.

THOMAS: And wine.

THOMAS and MARTIN leave.

Scene 11

ERIFILA: What do you think you're looking at?

FLORIANO: Even the moon and stars stare at you,
such is your beauty. Forgive me.
(*Aside.*) If I do not speak to her, I'll die,
but how can I make her understand.

ERIFILA: (*Aside.*) He has a fierce look in his eye;
I think he might be dangerous,
but I can't move. Not a muscle.
My fear won't let me speak to him,
and my will won't let me run away.

FLORIANO: (*Aside.*) I look into her eyes and drown.
What words can there be between us?

ERIFILA: (*Aside.*) What sort of creature then is he?
A blank mind in a perfect form.

FLORIANO: (*Aside.*) To see such beauty brought so low.

ERIFILA: (*Aside.*) A cathedral without its roof.

FLORIANO: (*Aside.*) A delightful chamber empty.
A marble statue with no life
of the spirit or of the mind.
Never was it truer that beauty
is judged by the eye, not the brain.
A blank mind in a perfect form.
Such beauty wasted by unreason.

ERIFILA: (*Aside.*) I don't think he can be violent;
but what a waste of human form;
a golden chalice full of air
when it could hold the finest wine.
God, I would lose my wits for him.

FLORIANO: (*Aside.*) The madhouse is a paradise,
and if this angel has fallen
then I'll fall to earth with her too.

ERIFILA: (*Aside.*) If only I dared speak to him
but the last vestige of reason
has bound my tongue with iron bands.

FLORIANO: (*Aside.*) How can the sane worship the mad?
And yet it is love and not death
which is the great leveller.

ERIFILA: (*Aside.*) I've just awoken from a dream
and I feel sleep arising again.
I've lived my whole life sunk in sleep,
everything has been done in dream.
Did I leave my father's house

without even a backward glance?
Who was it Leonato robbed?
Was it me that cried for vengeance
when a servant proved insulting?
My mind's on fire, my thoughts aflame,
and I no longer know myself.
I'm standing looking at a madman
knowing full well I'd follow him
to the ends of the earth if need be.
They'll have brought me to the madhouse
for some similar foolishness.
There can be no doubt about it:
it's as clear as day: I am insane.

FLORIANO: (*Aside.*) Her eyes are clouding with new rage,
two bright stars eclipsed by the moon.

ERIFILA: That's it! I'm mad, insane, possessed!

FLORIANO: Calm down, my love, control your thoughts.

ERIFILA: Those aren't the words of a madman.

FLORIANO: Mad only with love for you,
and I swear that I'll go madder.

ERIFILA: No, you must not say such things.

FLORIANO: (*Aside.*) Why hang on to my common sense,
like a drunkard to his last glass,
when the woman I love has none?

ERIFILA: (*Aside.*) If madness must be our common ground...
(*Aloud.*) A horse! A horse! Bring me a horse!
My kingdom and my eyes for a horse.
My lover Galahad awaits.

FLORIANO: Yes... a horse! I'll have a horse too!
And a sword and an axe and a...
and all the other bits and pieces.

(*Aside.*) *Alea iacta est.* I've crossed
the Rubicon of sanity,
swam through the cold waters of reason
drawn to the warmth of this new love.

ERIFILA: You there, come and hold my stirrup.

FLORIANO: Your wish is my command, my love.
Where is it?

ERIFILA: You're fondling my foot,
miserable squire. How dare you!

FLORIANO: A squire? I am a captive, like you.

ERIFILA: A captive? I am Guinevere.

FLORIANO: Shall I be your Lancelot?

ERIFILA: Lancelot is a shining bright,
the most handsome man I have known.
He looks at women and they melt,
but none tempts his vow of chastity.

FLORIANO: No, not Lancelot... I'm Sir... Sir
Orlando.

ERIFILA: Sir Orlando? You're black Mordred!

FLORIANO: I'm not black anyone, I swear.
I'll be any knight that you want,
the whole round table if need be.

ERIFILA: Galahad!

FLORIANO: My lovely Queen!

ERIFILA: And Gawain?

FLORIANO: He's green with envy.
Sorry, my learned little joke.
Once a scholar... of my love for you,
and dare I hope, of yours for me?

ERIFILA: You know Tristan?

FLORIANO: And Merlin too.

ERIFILA: They were good people and good times.

FLORIANO: Camelot was the place to be,
    my Queen.

ERIFILA: (*Aside.*) He has a ready wit.
    Either he's sane as any man
    or I've lost my senses utterly.

FLORIANO: (*Aside.*) I've been too clever for my own good.
    I think she's seen right through me.
    I'll have a frenzy of my own.
    (*Aloud.*) For Spain and for Santiago,
    into the valley of death I ride,
    cannon to the right, guns on the left.

ERIFILA: It's a far far better thing you do.

FLORIANO: *Dulce et decorum est.*

ERIFILA: *Atque in perpetuo frater.*

FLORIANO: *Pro patria mori.*

ERIFILA: *Hic, haec, hoc.*

FLORIANO: *Morituri te salutant.*

Scene 12

Enter PISANO.

PISANO: That's enough hocus pocus.
    Time for you to get your tunic on.
    And you, Orlando, leave her alone.
    I know what you loonies are like.
    You'd do it on the street corner
    like a couple of dogs in heat.

ERIFILA: It's you're the dog; you're Arthur's cur.

FLORIANO: Eh yes, that's what you are, all right.

PISANO: Got a little thing going, eh?
    You'll not see each other again
    until Carnival comes around.
    My heart bleeds for you.

ERIFILA: Hopefully
    to death.

PISANO: That's enough noise from you.
    Get inside.

ERIFILA: Farewell, my beautiful
    madman.

FLORIANO: Farewell, my beautiful
    madlady.

PISANO: (*Leading ERIFILA off.*) Come on then, walkies.

Scene 13

FLORIANO: My thoughts are tangled like a maze;
    a labyrinth that's built upon
    a bottomless pit; if I fall
    I'll have lost myself for ever.
    Reason can't check these spinning thoughts
    no more than a falling man
    may pull himself up by the braces.
    The sane man weeps, the madman laughs;
    for the course that I have chosen
    – though it's the course that's chosen me –
    will lead only to tears and pain,
    and yet I'd gladly lose my mind,
    kill every ounce of common sense,
    for that lovely creature, who has none.

Scene 14

Enter VALERIO.

VALERIO: I haven't come to visit you,
  since you've been here but half a day.
  Business of my own brings me here,
  a matter of life or death for me.

FLORIANO: What's wrong, Valerio, tell me.
  Have they found out I'm in here.

VALERIO: No one knows a thing, my friend,
  and I swear that no one will
  unless heaven conspires against us.
  I'm here because I've lost my mind.

FLORIANO: What's happened to you, Valerio?
  You're the most balanced man I know.
  But your illness is plain to see:
  it's in the pallor of your cheek,
  it's in the wildness of your eye.

VALERIO: Did you see that girl they brought in,
  crying that she'd been robbed and stripped?
  More beautiful than the order
  of the heavens and the planets,
  more lovely than the elements,
  than any living thing on earth...

FLORIANO: And this mad creature, is she yours?

VALERIO: Not yet, but I'm already hers.

FLORIANO: Let's find somewhere that we can talk,
  and we'll try to pluck this madness
  from your soul, before it's too late.

VALERIO: Floriano, it's too late now.
  The madness has consumed my soul.
  There's no cure, no miracle now.

How can a man tumbling through space
pull himself up by his own belt?
And why should he even want to try?

End of Act One.

ACT TWO

Scene 1

Enter FLORIANO.

FLORIANO: Fortune must have its little joke,
    piling despair upon despair
    so that the will eventually snaps.
    Sane or mad, we're fortune's playthings;
    I was snatched from the gates of death,
    and now I'm more dead than ever,
    tossed like a leaf in the heart's deep storm.
    She looked with a goddess's gaze,
    in her eyes flared madness and fire,
    and like a moth I flew too close,
    spinning madly into the flame.
    And when the storm in head and heart
    had fanned the fire into white heat,
    when I most needed time to think,
    to freeze the molten flow of thought,
    then the earth opened up below me.
    My greatest and dearest friend
    has been used by cruel fortune
    as her most outrageous arrow.
    Valerio, who gave me new hope,
    without whom I would now be dead,
    says that his life hangs from a thread,
    and that whether she's mad or sane
    he means to have her for his own.
    If he pretends she's a relative,
    then he'll be granted full licence
    to take her home. If I lose her,
    whether she's mad or if she's sane,
    then the only thing left to me
    will be the madness of the storm.

Scene 2

Enter FEDRA. She doesn't see FLORIANO.

FEDRA: I can't settle to anything;
    I've been wandering round this madhouse
    like a ghost without a castle,
    and my steps bring me here each time,
    to the place that I first saw him.
    Love has cut me down like a scythe,
    my senses now control my sense,
    and my whole being is possessed.
    They say that love is a madness,
    a fire that blazes within,
    but I am covered in fire
    and I would give myself to him,
    do anything with him, for him,
    to douse this fire in my brain,
    in my heart and in my body.

FLORIANO: (*Aside.*) Then we'll fight madness with madness.

FEDRA: (*Aside.*) Madness rises up to madness.
    It changes colour, changes form,
    like the artful chameleon,
    matching itself to its desire.

FLORIANO: I've lost something! It's quite, quite gone.
    I don't suppose that you've seen it?

FEDRA: I don't suppose that you've seen me,
    the torture and torment of my heart?

FLORIANO: You are beyond doubt a lady
    of noble sensibility
    that you should grieve so much for my loss.
    You'll get your reward in heaven,
    my daughter.

FEDRA: In heaven or hell,
    what difference does it make to me.
    My appetite is here and now.

FLORIANO: What you need is fresh goat's cheese.
    Help me find my favourite pebble
    and I'll give you some aubergines.
    Ho, everyone that thirsteth
    come ye to the waters and drink!

FEDRA: (*Aside.*) There's a fury in him I can't touch.

FLORIANO: And those who hath no money,
    let them come by too and eat.
    Bring me the brains of the Baptist!

FEDRA: If I could find your brains for you,
    I'd return them on a salver.

FLORIANO: Herodias! Jezabel! Whore!
    You've sent Salome to seduce me,
    to parade her cruel beauty
    in front of me and steal my mind.

FEDRA: And do you think me beautiful?
    I'd dance for you, undress for you.

FLORIANO: My love has teeth as white as pearls,
    and her lips as red as peppers;
    her kiss is like a burning jewel.
    I loved her once, I love her still.
    Get thee behind me, Salome.
    You can't tempt me. Your mouth is pus.

FEDRA: And for pearl-white teeth and red lips,
    you lost your mind?

FLORIANO: I lost my mind
    and in its place I found wisdom
    and then the devil appeared to me.
    And with the pact we made I lost...

FEDRA: What, my poor love?

FLORIANO: I don't remember.

FEDRA: Do you remember the ribbon,
    the green ribbon that I gave you?
    I said that it would bring you hope.

FLORIANO: I threw that hope back into the game,
    into the mad game we play here,
    and the ribbon just... disappeared.
    Fortune dealt me a better hand.

FEDRA: What better hand?

FLORIANO: We gamble here
    with stakes much higher than you think.
    A lifetime's hope and happiness
    on the single turn of a card.
    And I was dealt the Queen of Hearts...
    but now I see a Knave of Spades
    and he may win my Queen away.
    It's time to turn the card and see.

FEDRA: You'd gamble the hope I gave you?

FLORIANO: I'd gamble all the hope in the world,
    the hope of the future and the past.

FEDRA: Shall I give you another ribbon,
    in case you should just lose your Queen?

FLORIANO: I'll accept your ribbon gladly,
    but I may give it to my love.
    Where is it?

FEDRA: Here. Come and get it.
    Can't you see it?

FLORIANO: You take it off.

FEDRA: My hands are trembling. Untie it.

    FLORIANO begins to remove the ribbon from her throat.

(*Aside.*) Oh God, he's almost in my arms.
There's no reason now to hold back.
He's nothing but a witless fool.

FLORIANO: Get your hand out of my pocket!
You're trying to steal my pebbles!

FEDRA: (*Aside.*) Let me hold myself against you.
You've no sense of what's right or wrong;
why should any the more have I?

Scene 3

Enter ERIFILA, dressed in a hospital tunic and cap.

ERIFILA: I wish you both health and long life.
Here's the man who wanted to be
Lancelot to my Guinevere
who made Gawain go green with envy.
Just another lying bastard.
One of the pleasures of madness
is its freedom from all restraint.
So I think I'll say it again:
just another lying bastard.
And who do you think you are then?
What fairy tale have you sprung from?
Not the administrator's niece,
with more ribbons than a prize cabbage?
If you're sane, you're mad to be here;
his soul is sick, his mind twisted,
and you dance upon his every word.
You thrust yourself into his arms.

FEDRA: Now don't get angry, Elvira.

ERIFILA: Better get back to your uncle's,
or I'll change you into a toad.

FEDRA: (*Aside.*) They have the strength of seven men,
when the mood takes them. I'll just go.

Scene 4

FLORIANO: (*Aside.*) So it seems fortune's tide has turned.
    They say jealousy's the fruit of love;
    I'd say its root. It engenders
    the fiercest, most burning passion.
    (*Aloud.*) What melancholy's this, my Queen?

ERIFILA: I raised my voice to my mistress.
    My temper's as quick as the wind,
    and now you'll think that I love you
    when you're already in love with her.

FLORIANO: Elvira, on my mother's grave,
    and for all that's good and holy,
    if I've the least regard for her,
    let me be boiled alive in oil.
    And if I'm not Sir Lancelot,
    and Guinevere's devoted slave,
    then let me be roasted or fried.
    We were playing a game that's all,
    to see whether she likes butter,
    holding a flower to her chin.

ERIFILA: I think I'd prefer you roasted.
    Remember these words, Orlando.
    I came here and I looked at you.
    After you, I'll look at the wall.
    I don't believe your butter game,
    but I'll make you my Lancelot.

FLORIANO: (*Aside.*) Love, intervene for this woman
    and restore her senses to her;
    God take Fedra's if need be.

ERIFILA: (*Aside.*) Love, if you indeed echo heaven,
    give this man back what he has lost.

FLORIANO: (*Aside.*) Love, give back a soul to this face
    for she is a monster of beauty.

Make her able to understand
the great love that I feel for her.

ERIFILA: (*Aside.*) Love, shed some light into his mind
so that he can understand me.

FLORIANO: (*Aside.*) Otherwise, heaven help us both.

ERIFILA: (*Aside.*) How can I tell him who I am
if I cannot trust his reaction?

FLORIANO: (*Aside.*) If I cannot trust her reaction,
how can I tell her who I am?

ERIFILA: (*Aside.*) But the madwoman could tell him,
for who's to know it's not fantasy?

FLORIANO: (*Aside.*) The madman can speak the sane man's
thoughts.

ERIFILA: Let's talk together, you and I.

FLORIANO: About Camelot?

ERIFILA: About love.
What does love mean to you, good sir?

FLORIANO: The principle of creation,
a desire that's born through the eyes
and fires the mind and body:
the perfect balance of two souls.

ERIFILA: (*Aside.*) This isn't madness.

FLORIANO: The urge to have,
to possess, the beauty we see
and in whose image we are formed,
for all lovers are Narcissus.

ERIFILA: (*Aside.*) He speaks like a philosopher.
Ah, but that may be his obsession.

FLORIANO: And beauty itself is varied:
the beauty of appearances,
harmony of outer form,

which you have in great abundance,
though you don't understand a word;
and the beauty of the intellect,
distributed by St Peter
to those souls about to be born.
You must have been gazing at the moon
and missed the gifts he pressed upon you.

ERIFILA: Weigh your words with care, moonstruck fool.

FLORIANO: I'm no more the moon's fool than you.

ERIFILA: The moon affects me once a month.

FLORIANO: The moon is your sign, Elvira;
    all your brilliance is reflection.

ERIFILA: And your brain is the size of a...

FLORIANO: Planet.

ERIFILA: Jupiter or Mercury?

FLORIANO: (*Aside.*) This woman's clearly no one's fool.
    (*Aloud.*) And what do you know of love's sting?

ERIFILA: That we talk of being arrowstruck,
    that arrows are shot from bows like moons,
    that love is a form of madness.
    All of this I knew in theory
    until I met you in this place
    and I felt the sting in my flesh.
    The theory was turned into fact.

FLORIANO: You understand theory and fact?

ERIFILA: (*Aside.*) This man sounds as sane as I am.

FLORIANO: (*Aside.*) Who knows, she might have just struck
        lucky.

ERIFILA: Do you understand what I mean?
    That I like you, that you please me,

like pepper enriches red wine.

FLORIANO: Like bacon after Holy Week,
    like mutton on a Saturday.

ERIFILA: (*Aside.*) His wit's too quick for a madman.

FLORIANO: She's sane! More than sane, she has wit!

ERIFILA: I come from a noble family.

FLORIANO: Mine has many lands in the north.

ERIFILA: I ran away from my father
    with a servant who robbed and stripped me.

FLORIANO: They say I killed a man, a prince.

ERIFILA: He fled like a frightened whippet...

FLORIANO: I pretended to be insane...

ERIFILA: ... and got nothing from me but scorn.

FLORIANO: ... to keep my neck out of the noose.

ERIFILA: Are you telling me the truth?

FLORIANO: Yes.
    Are you?

ERIFILA: I swear I am, my love.
    Although I am not called Elvira
    nor am I as mad as you thought.
    Until they brought me here by mistake
    my name was Erifila
    and I was my father's darling.
    You can trust me with your secrets;
    I'll be as silent as the grave
    and I'll worship you until I die.

FLORIANO: The sky has opened up for me.
    Kiss me, Erifila.

ERIFILA: Oh yes,
    I give myself to you in madness.

Scene 5

Enter PISANO.

PISANO: I knew it. They're at it like dogs.
    Bring a bucket of cold water!

FLORIANO: You're jealous, Pisano, that's all.

PISANO: Just because you're out of your minds
    doesn't mean you're a pair of rabbits.
    I'll soon fix you. Martin! Thomas!

FLORIANO: (*Aside.*) Piling despair upon despair.

Scene 6

Enter MARTIN and THOMAS.

THOMAS: Moors on the coast! Man the cannon!

PISANO: All right, Thomas, take it easy.
    I want them to be kept apart.
    Hobble him and manacle her.
    If they can manage it after that,
    then they must be contortionists.

FLORIANO: It was my fault, so chain me up.

PISANO: It was your fault?

FLORIANO: Leave her alone!

PISANO: One more word, and it's the cage for you.

MARTIN: You were told when you arrived here:
    that men and women stay apart,
    until we go out for Carnival.

THOMAS: What sort of maniac are you?

PISANO: Get them out of my sight.

THOMAS: Mush! Mush!

ERIFILA: (*To PISANO.*) Don't think that I don't see your
game.
    I know that look that's in your eyes.

MARTIN and THOMAS lead off FLORIANO and ERIFILA.

Scene 7

PISANO: Mad attracts mad; natural enough.
    Like to like; birdbrains of a feather.
    But she churns the brains of the sane;
    my mind's spinning like a windmill
    left standing in a hurricane.
    At my age, nothing excited me
    beyond a glass of good red wine.
    And now I look at the mirror,
    I fix my hair, practice my smile,
    make sure my clothes are hanging well.
    This is the madness of seagulls
    wheeling and pitching on the wind.
    But I'd not change it for the world.

Scene 8

Enter THOMAS.

THOMAS: Pisano, there's a knight outside
    with... with...

PISANO: With what, Thomas, with what?

THOMAS: With an accent from Aragon.

PISANO: Tell him I've got one already.

THOMAS: Right!

    THOMAS makes to leave.

PISANO: Thomas, think straight. Who is it?

THOMAS: Your cousin from Zaragoza,
  the city constable, righter of...

PISANO: You mean Liberto?

THOMAS: Liberto!

PISANO: Then tell him to come in. Madmen...

Scene 9

Enter LIBERTO.

LIBERTO: How could I come to Valencia
  and not call in here to see you?
  Though you understand, my mission...

PISANO: Liberto, let me embrace you
  once and a thousand times over.

LIBERTO: My dear cousin, my dearest friend.

PISANO: You must consider this your home.

LIBERTO: What do you mean? That I'm insane?

PISANO: Simply that my home is your home.
  What business brings you to these parts?

LIBERTO: You've heard about Prince Reinero?

PISANO: Only some gossip here and there;
  some people say he's been murdered,
  others that he's safe in hiding,
  a lie cooked up for reasons of state.

LIBERTO: The state never lies, not ever!
  He's as dead as a piece of pork,
  and every constable in Spain
  has been dispatched to hunt his killer.
  But the less you know the better.

PISANO: Prince Reinero was a good man.
  The whole of Spain seeks justice done.

LIBERTO: Oh yes, we'll get him, mark my words.
  His mistress gave us his portrait
  and commended his soul to hell.
  We had a hundred copies made.
  But I don't want to say too much.

PISANO: Can I see?

LIBERTO: For a moment, yes.
  Bear in mind it's state property.

He hands him a portrait.

PISANO: It could be anyone... you or me.
  What does this say?

LIBERTO: Floriano,
  aetatis suae twenty-nine,
  perhaps thirty now. Remember
  appearances are deceptive.

PISANO: There's a gentle look in his eye.
  There's some of them in here
  would kill you soon as look at you.
  One of them, Orlando, believe...

LIBERTO: Is that loony there eavesdropping?
  My mission must remain secret.

PISANO: He's looking at the stars and moon
  and wondering where the sun's gone.
  He's as empty as a virgin's bed.
  Your secret will be safe with him.
  But we'll go to my apartments.
  No one will interrupt us there.

They leave.

Scene 10

THOMAS: The world's much too wide for secrets.
    Which is why they say walls have ears
    and what's known to one is known to all.
    If I knew what this secret meant
    I'd save the life of my best friend;
    like Don Quijote I'd ride out!

Scene 11

Enter FLORIANO, his legs hobbled.

FLORIANO: Now I've got no one to turn to.
    How do I get out of this place
    if I can't trust Valerio?
    By God, I'm talking to myself,
    a sure sign of insanity.
    What ho, good sir Thomas, my Lord!

THOMAS: Orlandito, my favourite squire.
    They've shackled you like a prize pig.

FLORIANO: The old lady's will, they call these,
    after the pitiful old crone
    who left her entire fortune
    to the prisons and castles of Spain.
    'Buy something for the prisoners',
    she stipulated. So they did.

THOMAS: The knave who killed Prince Reinero
    should be shackled and whipped instead.
    And they'll find him with that portrait.
    They'll not leave any stone unturned.

FLORIANO: Who told you?

THOMAS: Pisano's cousin.

FLORIANO: And did he show you the portrait?

THOMAS: The varlet's name began with 'Flor'.

FLORIANO: Floriano?

THOMAS: Maybe.

FLORIANO: What else?

THOMAS: He's thirty, give or take a year.

FLORIANO: Do they know where the... varlet... is?

THOMAS: By the hair of my beard, they don't.

FLORIANO: Where are they now?

THOMAS: They've gone inside.

FLORIANO: I've a mind to see that portrait.
    You wait here.

THOMAS: Don't say I told you.
    It's supposed to be a secret.

FLORIANO: I won't breathe a word to a soul.

THOMAS: Orlando, my favourite squire.

    Exit FLORIANO.

Scene 12

Enter ERIFILA, her wrists manacled.

ERIFILA: Thomas, what are you doing here?

THOMAS: My Lady, how did you escape?

ERIFILA: Martin was working on his book
    and he suddenly keeled over.

THOMAS: He does that; authors often do.
    If Pisano finds you out here
    he'll have your lovely guts for garters.

ERIFILA: He's already got me in chains
    like some rabid dog.

THOMAS: He'll beat you.
    Though God knows it would be a sin.

ERIFILA: Do you think I'm pretty, Thomas?

THOMAS: As pretty as the moon and stars,
    and if I weren't mad already...
    We could get married so we could!
    I'm...

ERIFILA: Martin says you're Don Quijote.

THOMAS: I say that to keep him happy.
    Because if I'm not Don Quijote
    then how can he be Cervantes?
    It's simple. I'm the King of Spain.

ERIFILA: Then I pledge to your majesty...

THOMAS: What? What?

ERIFILA: That I will marry you.

THOMAS: Now?

ERIFILA: When broken shells make Christmas bells.

THOMAS: I don't want to wait to Christmas!

ERIFILA: Well, if there was a priest here now...

THOMAS: A priest? I'll fetch a cardinal!

ERIFILA: Orlando has taken orders!
    Go and find him. He'll marry us.

THOMAS: Give me your hand.

ERIFILA: My hands are chained.

THOMAS: By God, I'll free you from your chains!

ERIFILA: Just go and look for Orlando.

THOMAS: Orlando, my favourite squire,
a priest... who would have believed it?
You'll be a cardinal, my boy!

Exit THOMAS.

Scene 13

ERIFILA: By the time he finds Orlando,
he'll have forgotten what he wants.
Orlando, my love, I want you.
I've never loved another man,
felt the slightest stirring in my soul,
till we met in this asylum.
I watched Leonato sleeping
every night, not closing my eyes
in case he came into my bed,
hating his touch upon my skin
when he tried to draw me to him,
thinking I'd never give myself
to any man. I want you now.
This madness has become my soul.

Scene 14

Enter FLORIANO, his face blacked up.

FLORIANO: Elvira.

ERIFILA: Floriano... what...

FLORIANO: A wise philosopher once said
that life is like a game of chess,
that white becomes black overnight,
that intellect must play with passion.
A king with his one hundred pawns
moves relentlessly down the board
to take one piece, a single knight.

He sends his castle before him,
a rook to put the knight in check,
before the king closes in for mate.
But what if the white knight turns black?

ERIFILA: What do you mean a rook has come?

FLORIANO: I've heard that he has a portrait.

ERIFILA: I don't think I like this game.

FLORIANO: No,
but you're a part of it as well,
a queen who can pluck her knight from death.

ERIFILA: What exactly is happening?
Nobody's listening; speak clearly.

FLORIANO: One of Reinero's men is here,
and he has a likeness of me.

ERIFILA: Then hide.

FLORIANO: He must see the madman,
and seeing the madman, forget me.

ERIFILA: Your secret proves your love for me,
and I'll help you, though it costs my life.
Without you, my love, I have no life.

FLORIANO: So they put chains on you as well.

ERIFILA: Not chains, jewels in the eyes of love.

FLORIANO: Love has made us one prisoner,
bound and chained both hand and foot.

ERIFILA: The chains around your feet, my love,
I wear them willingly round my heart.
If only my arms could open
to draw you closer to my breast.

FLORIANO: I hear footsteps!

ERIFILA: Shall I stay or go?

FLORIANO: Stay... it's too late now anyway.

Scene 15

Enter PISANO and LIBERTO.

LIBERTO: I must get to Alicante
  before Friday.

PISANO: You won't stay then?

LIBERTO: I'll take no rest till I find him,
  and I'll hardly do that in here.

PISANO: What do you two think you're doing?

FLORIANO: You treat me with rough injustice,
  more so in the dubious company
  of this ruffian. What do you want?
  I know that you want to hurt me!

ERIFILA: Who are you? Go on, who are you?

LIBERTO: I am here on the King's business,
  in search of a dangerous man.
  It's better you don't know too much.

FLORIANO: There are a hundred such men here.

ERIFILA: What did he do, this dangerous man?

LIBERTO: He killed a prince.

ERIFILA: And what's his name,
  this dangerous man?

LIBERTO: Floriano.

ERIFILA: A beautiful name. I'm his wife.

LIBERTO: You could find yourself in trouble,
  going around making claims like that.
  I'm on official state business.
  I am the King's representative.

PISANO: We have to watch this little one;
　　butter wouldn't melt in her mouth,
　　but deep down... lovely, though, isn't she?

ERIFILA: Why doesn't the King find my jewels?

PISANO: Stolen jewels – that's her obsession.

FLORIANO: Because the King has been robbed too.

ERIFILA: Who robbed the King?

FLORIANO:　　　　　　　　　I robbed the King!

ERIFILA: That's all right then. You're my prisoner.
　　I have you in chains already.
　　Speak! What did you steal from the King?

FLORIANO: His crown. Then I looked for his sceptre...

ERIFILA: Sceptre?

FLORIANO:　　Sceptre I couldn't find it.

ERIFILA: Will you give the King's jewels to me?

FLORIANO: Elvira, the crowned head of my heart.

LIBERTO: I warn you... I'm the King's agent.

FLORIANO: Speak of the devil and you get
　　his monkey riding on your back.

PISANO: Neither of them know what they're saying.
　　Pay no attention, Liberto.

FLORIANO: Do you have the slightest idea
　　of who I am or what I've done?

LIBERTO: I know you think you've robbed the King.
　　I know what your game is, my lad.
　　You're the sort that loves confessing;
　　you'd confess to killing Abel
　　if you thought that I'd arrest you.

FLORIANO: I'm going to throw the monkey off.
Do you know why my face is black?

LIBERTO: To match your humour, probably.
Or your soul, if loonies have one.

FLORIANO: It's to make people notice me,
like singing off-key in a choir.

ERIFILA: It's so that he can win at chess.

PISANO: Any more and you're in the cage!
(*To LIBERTO.*) Orlando will be here for life,
but Elvira leaves tomorrow.

ERIFILA: Where?

PISANO: You haven't heard the news?
Your cousin wants to take you home;
he's assumed responsibility
for your mental and physical care.

ERIFILA: Cousin?

FLORIANO: Cousin Valerio,
perhaps?

PISANO: So you know her cousin?

ERIFILA: It will be the blackest of days
before I eat and sleep in his house.
I prefer my honest madness
to his mealy-mouthed sanity!
Who would be cured by a liar?
I'd rather be locked in your cages!

LIBERTO: I can see you have your hands full.

PISANO: She rants and raves incessantly
and never makes a drop of sense.

FLORIANO: They told me you have a portrait.

LIBERTO: What portrait? What do you know?

FLORIANO: A portrait of the King of Spain.

LIBERTO: Would you like to see it, madman?

FLORIANO: I'd like nothing better in this world.

LIBERTO: Then look and tell me who it is.

He hands him the portrait.

FLORIANO: I know this face... and where he is.

LIBERTO: Of course you do.

FLORIANO: Just set me free
and I'll tell you where to find him.

LIBERTO: I've wasted enough time already.
Pisano, I must take my leave.

PISANO: I'll walk with you into the town.

LIBERTO: To tell you the truth, I'd welcome
some normal conversation.
I don't know how you keep sane in here.

PISANO and LIBERTO leave.

Scene 16

ERIFILA: If ever I doubted you were mad,
I take it all back; you're deranged!

FLORIANO: But the King's man will not be back.
This is one stone that's not been turned,
because it's turned itself for him.
Tell me, where's the madness in that?

ERIFILA: My heart was bursting in my mouth.

FLORIANO: Your heart was beating inside me.

ERIFILA: Must I still call you Orlando?

FLORIANO: My real name is Floriano.

ERIFILA: Floriano.

FLORIANO: Erifila.

ERIFILA: I thought you'd gone too far.

FLORIANO: How can a madman go too far?

ERIFILA: If I could I would hold you now...

FLORIANO: I've never felt freer in my life.
    My mind is free, my hands are free.

Scene 17

Enter LAIDA.

LAIDA: Thank God I came down when I did.
    Get your filthy hands off her!
    Leave her alone, you maniac!

ERIFILA: Who is this damsel – of sorts?

LAIDA: It's not your legs you should have chained.
    Why are you so obsessed with her?

FLORIANO: Because she looks at me with fire.

LAIDA: Then look somewhere else, Orlando.
    At me, for example.

ERIFILA: At you?
    Why should he want to look at you?
    You're coarse, dull, with the face of a cow.
    I'll call you Daisy.

FLORIANO: I am a knight
    who pays homage to his lady.

LAIDA: Homage. It looked more like a grope.

ERIFILA: Why don't you go and get yourself milked?

LAIDA: Orlando! Will you just stand by

and let this madwoman insult me?

ERIFILA: Lancelot, Guinevere is bored.
    Stay with your Daisy in distress,
    your dazzling bovine beauty.
    Her onion breath's too much for me.

FLORIANO: I'll go with you to Camelot,
    my Lady. Let Daisy graze here.

ERIFILA and FLORIANO leave.

Scene 18

LAIDA: I've been outwitted by half wits,
    with not a right thought between them.
    God help me, I love a madman,
    who prefers a madwoman to me.
    There's no dignity, no joy, in that.
    Yet their madness fits hand in glove
    and I cannot understand their world,
    or break their circle of delusion.
    But if I could, he would love me,
    he would love me and cast aside
    his Guinevere of ice and snow
    for the fire of my eyes and heart.

Scene 19

Enter FEDRA.

FEDRA: Laida, what brings you back down here?
    As if I didn't know.

LAIDA: Laida?

FEDRA: The most terrible thing's happened.

LAIDA: (*Singing.*) Volare, cantare, oh oh oh oh.

FEDRA: My whole world's gone, at one fell swoop.
    My uncle's sending me away.

My father's written from Madrid
ordering me home at once.
There's someone wants to marry me.

LAIDA: An old man with an old man's lance,
not a knight with burning lips.

FEDRA: Laida, it's not your place to spec...

LAIDA: I am the whore of Camelot.
I know Arthur's deepest secrets.
I've lain with Galahad and Merlin.

FEDRA: What's got into you. Stop screeching!

LAIDA: What's got into me? Anyone
and everyone. I know who I am.
I am the whore of Camelot!

FEDRA: Laida, you're not yourself today.

LAIDA: Where's the drink you were to bring me?
I told you to bring some sweet wine.
Wench, I'll teach you to obey.

FEDRA: If you think you can talk to me...

LAIDA: I'll have you flogged till you drop,
my ugly little serving maid.

FEDRA: You're mad. She's gone mad, she must have.
She's lost her wits.

LAIDA: I've found my wits!
I looked into his eyes and drank.

FEDRA: Pull yourself together.

LAIDA: Drop dead.
Volare, cantare, oh oh oh oh.

FEDRA: (*Aside.*) Her madness holds the key to him.
My Mistress, your wish is my command.

LAIDA: I've been kept waiting overlong.

82

FEDRA: The kitchen lad broke the bottle.

LAIDA: Then have him whipped very soundly.
　　　Unless you want him for yourself.
　　　(*Aside.*) What does she think she's playing at?

FEDRA: You'll not harm a hair on his head!
　　　He's Lancelot's favourite squire.

LAIDA: You dare mention my lover's name?
　　　Your filthy lips frame his fine name?
　　　With your snake's tongue, your pig's snout, you...

FEDRA: Fool, whore, don't you know we're married?

LAIDA: (*Aside.*) She's seen through me. (*Aloud.*) Who
　　　　　　　　　　　　　　　　　　　　married you?

FEDRA: The Pope. (*Aside.*) I envy her madness,
　　　but by following her frenzy
　　　they'll let me stay in the madhouse too.
　　　(*Aloud.*) The Pope of Rome in his white suit.

LAIDA: (*Aside.*) She's playing the same game as me.
　　　(*Aloud.*) I'll buy a rope to hang your pope
　　　and I'll have Lancelot instead.

FEDRA: Lancelot wouldn't spit on you
　　　even though you were dying of thirst.
　　　You're just another ugly servant.
　　　(*Aside.*) In madness veritas. Why not?

LAIDA: You'd be too frightened to lie with him.
　　　You're frigid, you're like death warmed up,
　　　you're as cold as a piece of fish,
　　　too stuck up to have it stuck up.
　　　(*Aside.*) Now we're really telling it straight.

FEDRA: Bring me an axe and I'll kill her!

LAIDA: I'll rearrange your face for you!

FEDRA: Lying whore!

LAIDA: Frigid bitch!

They fight.

Scene 20

Enter SANCHO, the Administrator of the asylum, and VALERIO.

SANCHO: You must excuse me, Valerio.
I think that's the matter settled,
but this fracas's driving me insane.

VALERIO: It seems we got here just in time.
There's a madwoman at your niece's throat.

SANCHO: Good God, Fedra! What's going on?
Hey you, let her go! What's your name?
Pisano! Pisano! Come here!
Get this shrew back into her cage!

LAIDA: Ah, the wicked witch's uncle.
Don't you recognise me, Sancho?

SANCHO: Laida! I can't believe my eyes.
Or my ears. You forget yourself.

FEDRA: This foul-mouthed slut, this two-faced whore
says that Orlando is her lover.

SANCHO: Impossible!

FEDRA: Of course it is.
Everyone knows he's my husband.
'A poor thing, señora, but your own',
he told me in our wedding bed.
He's always been a great scholar.

SANCHO: Fedra! Calm down! What's this about?

VALERIO: Don't you recognise your own trade,
Sancho? They're both as mad as hares.

FEDRA: Her love has got a red red nose.

LAIDA: You thought I was your niece's maid?
    Little man, how little you know.
    I am the Queen of Sheba.
    Look at my breast. It's burnt with love.

FEDRA: My breast too is covered with ash,
    where he has laid his hands and lips.

SANCHO: For the last time, control yourselves!

VALERIO: Someone has cast a spell on them.

SANCHO: This is not a spell or potion.
    I've seen the ravages of love
    work to evil effect before.
    I've made it a special study
    and published a treatise on this:
    Dr Sancho's Ars Curandi:
    Antidotes to Ars Amandi.
    I'll give you a copy later.

VALERIO: Thank you. So you can cure them?

SANCHO: No.
    The madness has to run its course.
    It was a black, black day you brought
    your mad friend to this asylum.

FEDRA: Everyone's sad. Let's have a dance.

SANCHO: Things are going from bad to worse.

    FEDRA and LAIDA dance.

VALERIO: I think you'd better lock them up
    before anyone else sees them.
    Think of your niece's reputation.
    Perhaps finding themselves in a cage
    will restore them to their senses.

SANCHO: By God, I'll kill them or cure them.
And when I've finished with your friend,
he'll wish that he'd never been born.
Advanced methods are well and good,
but when it comes to a crisis...

VALERIO: If he knew what he was doing,
if he was in his right mind, yes.
But you can't punish a madman
for actions beyond his control.

SANCHO: I'm in charge of this asylum!
He's been the root cause of all this.

FEDRA: If you hurt him, I'll kill myself,
I swear I will.

Scene 21

Enter PISANO, accompanied by THOMAS and MARTIN.

PISANO: You called me, sir.
I brought these two along in case.
Is there trouble?

SANCHO: Of the worst sort.

PISANO: Mistress Fedra, what are you doing?

FEDRA: I'm waiting to see my husband.

LAIDA: Yours! He's mine!

FEDRA: Easily explained.
You're mad.

LAIDA: You're the crazy one.

THOMAS: They're both clearly very disturbed.

SANCHO: They're both married to Orlando.
I'll soon rid them of that notion.

MARTIN: My beautiful Laida, married!
    I'll never write another word.

LAIDA: You'd do well to keep out of this
    or Orlando will run you through.

PISANO: Sanity's a fragile thing, sir.
    And Orlando's a dangerous man.
    But they'll be safe enough in my care.

SANCHO: And not a word to anyone.

PISANO: Take them.

THOMAS: Stand still.

FEDRA: You come near me
    and my husband'll flay you alive.

LAIDA: My husband!

FEDRA: He's mine! We're married!

*They close on one another again as THOMAS and MARTIN
struggle to control them.*

SANCHO: It's a pitiful spectacle
    that love should bring human beings so low.

VALERIO: And now, about my madwoman...
    when can I have her home with me?

End of Act Two.

ACT THREE

Scene 1

A room in the asylum. SANCHO and VERINO, a learned doctor.

VERINO: I'm worried she's not taking solids.
　　By fair means or foul, by hook or crook,
　　make sure she eats every day.
　　Then with Godspeed and a fair wind
　　her humours will trickle into place.

SANCHO: She hasn't eaten for two days,
　　ever since we put her in the cage.

VERINO: I suspected that from the outset.
　　She's suffering from atrophy,
　　collapse through lack of nourishment;
　　the stomach shrivels like a dry prune,
　　like a piece of fruit in the sun,
　　and then grows cold so the body
　　freezes in its extremities.
　　Press some vinegar to her nose
　　or even better, some warm bread,
　　and then plunge her elbows and feet
　　into bowls of boiling water.
　　There's no doubt, that'll do the trick;
　　she'll be up and about in a flash.

SANCHO: Can you treat her melancholy?

VERINO: Ah yes, I saw that from the start.
　　It's a form of catalepsis,
　　when the melancholic humours
　　blow hot throughout the body,
　　like the sirocco from Algery.
　　The ancients termed it 'erotes',
　　viz: the erotic obsession
　　which drives your niece's waking thoughts.

Sorry, not delicately put,
I'm afraid, but there it is.
The lovesick; a common ailment
in which the senses rise up,
leading to fits of wildest fury.
But we'll have her back on her feet
before you can say 'catatonia'.

SANCHO: Her fits have become worse of late.

VERINO: Ah, that was always in the runes.
   Posidonios of Athens
   discovered that the membranes swell,
   constricting the supply of blood
   to the equitable humours.
   There are a thousand and one cures;
   as many as we've had hot dinners,
   you and I, but there's one danger:
   remove the madman from her sight
   and your niece will surely die.

SANCHO: How can I keep them together?

VERINO: Ah, I see you follow my drift.
   You must go to her and pander.

SANCHO: Pander?

VERINO: Yes, to her obsession.
   Tell her she will indeed marry
   the object of her delusion.
   We turn to nature for our cure,
   to the natural principle
   that woman forms herself in man
   as matter itself seeks out form.

SANCHO: Marrying Orlando would cure her?

VERINO: As surely as day follows night.
   She would return to her first sense,
   shattered by her late obsession.

I quote from the Master Galen:
'Lock ye not the madman away
for melancholy grows apace
with darkness and with solitude.'
His meaning is, I think, crystal clear.

SANCHO: Indeed. You mean...

VERINO: What day is it?

SANCHO: Tuesday... Shrove Tuesday!... Carnival!

VERINO: When all Valencia celebrates.
    Let them join the celebrations
    to disperse those grey dense vapours
    and then we'll feed her heart's desire.
    We'll marry them this afternoon.
    By night she'll be as right as rain.

SANCHO: There's no question of a wedding night.

VERINO: The subject is, of course, delicate.
    Have no fear. Feed her obsession
    and her sanity is assured.

SANCHO: Talk of the devil... and here's his monkey.

VERINO: Monkey?

SANCHO: Orlando's coming down.

Scene 2

Enter FLORIANO, muttering.

FLORIANO: They can do what they will to me,
    kill me, hang, draw and quarter me,
    but they're not going to make me go.

SANCHO: What's worrying you, Orlando?

FLORIANO: Pisano wants me to go out
    to beg for alms this afternoon.

90

SANCHO: We do it every carnival;
    the inmates look forward to it.

VERINO: That's precisely what Galen meant.
    To the drunkard, wine; the madman, air.

FLORIANO: It's the shame of it, with madmen,
    parading up and down the street
    when I'm saner than any of you
    – and better educated too.
    I'm not going out to be gawped at.

SANCHO: Pisano! Pisano!

PISANO: (*Voice off.*)   Yes sir!

SANCHO: You can let Orlando stay here.

FLORIANO: (*To Verino.*) I don't think I've had the pleasure.

VERINO: You don't remember your old friends?

FLORIANO: No! Who are you?

VERINO: I'm the doctor.
    I saw you when you first came in.

FLORIANO: Good sir, good sir, I'm delighted
    to make your acquaintance again;
    the company of learned men
    sits well with me; men of science
    who know the very soul of things.

VERINO: Let me talk to you, my poor boy.
    Do you know what the word 'soul' means?

FLORIANO: The soul is both the prime mover
    and the perfection of the body.

VERINO: If I said 'heart', what word would you say?
    What word comes straight into your mind?

FLORIANO: 'Less'.

VERINO: Less heart?

SANCHO: Heartless.

VERINO: Ah, heartless.
    Chains?

FLORIANO: Balls.

VERINO: Balls?

SANCHO: Balls and chains, doctor.

VERINO: Ah, balls and chains. Very good. In?

FLORIANO: Sane.

VERINO: Out?

FLORIANO: Of your minds, all of you.

VERINO: Marry?

FLORIANO: Who?

VERINO: I'll ask the questions.
    Fedra?

FLORIANO: You've got to be joking!

VERINO: This is a fairly new technique;
    I don't think much of it myself
    and I doubt if it will catch on.
    But one thing has become quite clear!
    This man talks as though he were sane,
    even though he's obviously mad.
    It's a curious condition,
    though not unknown, and with Godspeed...

SANCHO: The doctor's mention of Fedra
    was not as idle as it seemed.
    My niece has gone out of her mind
    because of her great love for you.

VERINO: We propose that you marry her
    in an attempt to restore her wits.

FLORIANO: Do you mean really marry her?

SANCHO: (*Aside to VERINO.*) What should we say?

VERINO: It's carnival;
    tell him it'll be make-believe.

SANCHO: No, it will be just make-believe.
    That will be enough to cure her.
    And we'll be suitably grateful.

FLORIANO: In that case, how can I refuse?

SANCHO: I'll send for you when we're ready.

FLORIANO: I await your call, good doctors.

    SANCHO and VERINO leave.

Scene 3

FLORIANO: At least I don't have to go out
    and show myself in the city.
    Apart from the embarrassment,
    which is no small consideration,
    it could still be dangerous for me.
    It's my life not my sanity
    that's still in play; but locked away,
    my secret remains within these walls.
    God knows what secrets they have seen,
    and what secrets they have kept silent.

Scene 4

Enter ERIFILA.

ERIFILA: I've been looking for you, Orlando,
    to give you my congratulations,

even though they stick in my throat.
May you have and hold your Fedra
for a thousand years to come.

FLORIANO: News travels fast in the madhouse.

ERIFILA: Fedra's shouting it from the rooftops.

FLORIANO: Don't let anger blind your good sense.
This is just make-believe, nothing more.
You should be laughing, not angry;
it's Fedra's the dupe, not you.

ERIFILA: So you think this is amusing?
This is a trifle to be laughed at?
From now on, you're a married man!

FLORIANO: Married?

ERIFILA: That's what a wedding does.
It marries you.

FLORIANO: No it doesn't.
I'm not getting married for real.

ERIFILA: You've agreed to the arrangements.

FLORIANO: The arrangements are real enough
but the intention is to cure her;
we'll be no more married than the priest,
and even he will be a fake.
There's nothing to worry about.
It's a good deed; just play-acting.

ERIFILA: So you think love is mere theatre,
that the soul is a laughing-stock?
Yesterday you pledged your soul to me.

FLORIANO: My love, may God strike me down dead
if I've spoken an untrue word;
may my heart which is yours burst wide,
may all my hopes be turned to dust

and my peace be consumed by war.
My day rises and sets with you,
and you can plunge me into darkness,
but I swear that I haven't lied.

ERIFILA: Now I know that Fedra's your wife.
Your protestations are fuelled by guilt
and trip too lightly off the tongue.
There's not a single word of truth
in anything you've said to me,
except today's your wedding day.
What did I ever ask from you?
We asked, we owe, each other nothing;
I gave you nothing and God knows
it's nothing that I take away.
Yesterday we met, today we part;
there's nothing more to be said for us.
Was it you took me from my home?
Was it you brought me to this land?
What have you ever done for me?
What services or tokens of love
have you ever pressed upon me?
And just what difference will it make
on earth, in heaven or in hell,
whether you marry her or me?
I've no reason to call you cruel;
you've simply flattered to deceive.
I've no right to stop your marriage
for I've played my own part in this charade,
and I'll atone in my own way.
So from now on, false Orlando
I wash my hands of you. For good.

FLORIANO: Love's not a stain to be washed away
nor a sin to be cleansed by water.
Heaven will bring you back to me,
for though our love's barely days old
I've held you in my heart for years,

through the shades and mysteries of the soul.
Philosophy tells us time and space
are folds on destiny's dark robe.
We are the linchpin of time and space,
upon which countless angels dance.
We are cast in the image of stars,
in the guiding stars of our love.
And in our two days of desire
we have known and loved each other
for a hundred – a thousand! – years.

ERIFILA: Always the bloody philosopher!
I'd rather talk to the simplest fool
than listen to your false science,
to your bluster and your breeze.

FLORIANO: Then what words will you listen to?
That my soul is frozen with fear,
that my heart is burning with fire,
that hell has opened at my feet
and that I balance on the edge.
Only say the word and I'll fall
or now that fortune's freed your hands
hold out your arms, Erifila,
and your husband will live again.

ERIFILA: You do not realise how contempt
is born quickly from betrayal.
I could not hold out my arms to you
were you drowning and crying to me.

FLORIANO: I know you well, Erifila.
I know your heart is full of love.

ERIFILA: Leave me alone!

FLORIANO: My love!

ERIFILA: Your love?

FLORIANO: I love you.

ERIFILA: You're marrying her.

FLORIANO: There's a hollowness within me.

ERIFILA: I'm sure Fedra will fill it well.

FLORIANO: I want you.

ERIFILA: You've asked for Fedra.

FLORIANO: You're crying; are your tears false too?

ERIFILA: What tears? You've turned my eyes to stone.

FLORIANO: I'll kill myself.

ERIFILA: I'll get the sword.

FLORIANO: Do you mean it?

ERIFILA: Do you mean it?

FLORIANO: Just say the word, I'll cut my throat.

ERIFILA: You'd be doing yourself a favour
    if you simply cut out your tongue.
    You allow it to wag too much.
    You've let it say yes to Fedra.

FLORIANO: You want me to cut out my tongue
    to spite your face.

ERIFILA: Someone's coming.

VALERIO: (*Voice off.*) Don't worry, I can manage her.
    I've got a couple of servants
    waiting for me outside the gates.

FLORIANO: Of all people, Valerio!
    He's coming for you.

ERIFILA: I hope he is.

FLORIANO: You won't go.

ERIFILA: Just watch me and see.

Scene 5

Enter VALERIO.

VALERIO: I've come to take you home with me.

ERIFILA: Dear cousin, I rejoice to see you.

VALERIO: How goes it with you. Orlando?

FLORIANO: In God's truth, things couldn't be worse.

VALERIO: I don't think you've got room for complaint.
Did you hear I got the licence?

ERIFILA: And I give thanks to God for it.

FLORIANO: And God knows how happy that makes me.

VALERIO: She'll want for nothing in my house.

FLORIANO: Except her sanity.

VALERIO: I'll cure her.

FLORIANO: And what will you expect from her?

VALERIO: It's not right to abandon her here.
I've thought about nothing else since,
so much I've started to believe
that she really is my cousin.

ERIFILA: When I leave this place, this madhouse,
I'll shake the dust from off my feet.
I hear they're having a wedding,
that there'll be lots of fireworks
for a marriage that's made in hell,
a marriage of carnival fools.
Take me home, good Valerio.

VALERIO: You'll see the wedding after all,
for Don Sancho's invited me.
Though who the bride and bridegroom are...

ERIFILA: Who cares! With you by my side,
kind Valerio, we'll see them married,
and with you I feel my fury wane.

FLORIANO: (*Aside to ERIFILA.*) Yours is the cold fury of
the sane.

ERIFILA: (*Aside to FLORIANO.*) An eye for an eye, my true
love.

FLORIANO: (*Aside to ERIFILA.*) You go to a greater
prison,
where your feelings are kept locked away.
If that's what you want, so be it.
But the madhouse will still be here,
and you can always come back home
or you can stay away for ever.

ERIFILA: Valerio, take me away.

VALERIO: I've a sedan chair at the gate.

FLORIANO: (*Aside.*) As soon as the gates slam behind her,
she'll be sorry. (*Aloud.*) So you're going?

ERIFILA: Gladly.

FLORIANO:　　　We'll miss you.

VALERIO:　　　　　　　　Goodbye, my friend.
I must get her home while I can.
I'll come back later.

ERIFILA:　　　　　　I shall not.
(*Aside to FLORIANO.*) Goodbye for ever. You're a fool.
It's your wife now I feel pity for.

FLORIANO: (*Aside to ERIFILA.*) When an angel passes us by
it's always a consolation
to have a bottle of wine to hand,
to keep the lonely cold at bay.

ERIFILA: (*Aside to FLORIANO.*) I'm sure you'll soon drink
Fedra dry.

FLORIANO: (*Aside to ERIFILA.*) You'll be the sorry one, my
love.

ERIFILA: (*Aside to FLORIANO.*) Well, you'll be too drunk to
notice.

FLORIANO: (*Aside to ERIFILA.*) Off you go, like a frightened
lamb

in the hands of the butcher's boy.

VALERIO leads ERIFILA away.

Scene 6

FLORIANO: All that fury, all that frenzy,
were simply the blustering of love.
Suspicion, jealousy and love
make for passionate bedfellows.
But I had to swallow love and pride
because Valerio was there,
because I still owe him my life
and because my life depends on him.
I feel her absence already,
crawling like a presence on my flesh,
but she'll be back. I know she will.
Love cannot die so easily.
Meanwhile let's sit back and wait
to see what this sham wedding brings.

Exit FLORIANO.

Scene 7

Enter PISANO, brandishing a whip. He cracks it around LAIDA, THOMAS, MARTIN, BELARDO (a madman who thinks he is Lope de Vega), MORDACHO and other inmates. Several of them sing in foreign languages. Bedlam.

PISANO: Not an offensive word or look
    from any of you, is that clear?
    No touching yourselves or each other.
    We're here to make people happy,
    make them go on their way with a smile,
    digging deep into their pockets.
    Right, off you go. We need the money.

MARTIN: Alms, for pity's sake, give us alms.

BELARDO: Charity for poor lunatics.

MORDACHO: Do, re, me, fa, so, la, te, do.

LAIDA: This madness is taking hold of me.
    I must remember not to forget
    that I'm sane. I mustn't forget
    to remember.   To remember...

MORDACHO: Man and woman are music; life,
    the stars, the moon, the sun, the sky;
    the planets, the zodiac, all things
    contain music within themselves.
    Music is the beauty of things.
    La musique avant toute chose.
    Do, re, me, fa, so, la, te, do.

BELARDO: Poetry if it is to be such,
    and song is merely a lesser form,
    must combine passion with instruction,
    music with a sense of purpose,
    pleasing the ear, speaking to the mind.

MARTIN: Alms, for pity's sake, give us alms.

BELARDO: Charity for poor lunatics.

LAIDA: Orlando's eyes are deepest blue,
    like the deepest lake I ever saw.
    I think I drowned in them once.

THOMAS: Alms! Who'll give alms to these poor souls?

PISANO: Look into your hearts and deeper
    into your pockets, good townsfolk.

Scene 8

Enter a GENTLEMAN, in travelling clothes.

GENTLEMAN: Miserable wretches. Who are they?

PISANO: Loonies.

GENTLEMAN: So a... a... what is the noun
    for madmen?

PISANO: A chaos perhaps.

GENTLEMAN: Indeed, a chaos of madmen.

PISANO: From the city asylum, sir.

GENTLEMAN: The marvel of all Valencia
    is its asylum, I've heard tell.
    Zaragoza's, in comparison,
    languishes in the dark ages.
    One of the seven wonders, I'm told,
    of human charity in this world.
    The crowning glory of the city.
    It would be a pity to leave
    without having visited it,
    without seeing its poor inmates
    in their own sauce, so to speak.
    Are they always as quiet as this?

PISANO: They've all been receiving treatment.

Some of them were... well, quite violent.

GENTLEMAN: Were they indeed. And you cured them?
Who's he?

PISANO: He was a musician, sir,
who one day found he couldn't write
or sing anything but the scale.

GENTLEMAN: And him?

PISANO: We call him Belardo.
He says he's a famous poet,
that in his lifetime he has lived
a hundred lives and has written
well over two thousand plays,
novels, epics and pastorals,
that he sailed with the Armada
and looked upon Ireland's green shore,
that he was exiled from the Court
and visited by the Inquisition,
that in time he became a priest
and has fathered fifty children,
that he has known the madness of love.

GENTLEMAN: Those of us still in our right minds
should give thanks to God for His mercy.

BELARDO: The madhouse, sir, is a godless place
and all the ills of this false world
are visited here. No one escapes.

GENTLEMAN: No one?

BELARDO: No one can cast stones,
because there's no one so intact
they don't carry some act of madness,
some terrible insanity
in their memory or in their mind.
Who can say they know who they are?

GENTLEMAN: This man is some kind of sorcerer.

PISANO: They say he was a great scholar,
    both of the arts and of the stars.

MORDACHO: Do, re, me, fa, so, la, te, do.
    Was that how the concerto goes?
    God help me, I can't remember.

PISANO: I can see, sir, you're fascinated.

GENTLEMAN: I would see more of this wondrous place.

PISANO: In that case, come this afternoon.
    You'll see something you'll never forget.
    Two of them are getting married.

GENTLEMAN: Then I'll come as your guest, my friend.

PISANO: My honour and privilege, sir.

GENTLEMAN: Take this as a sign of my thanks.

PISANO: May God repay your kindness, sir.
    Come to the asylum at five.
    You won't forget this day, I promise.
    Right, you lot.

LAIDA: Orlando, I love you!

MORDACHO: I remember semi-quavers!

THOMAS: The whole wide world's a madhouse.

MARTIN: But it's all quietly covered up.

BELARDO: Why should there be only nine muses
    when there are nine thousand poets?
    Why should there be only nine muses
    when every madness has its own?

They shuffle off.

Scene 9

A yard inside the hospital. SANCHO and VERINO.

SANCHO: The cure has been miraculous!
As soon as she heard they'd be married,
she ate, she drank, she spoke, she slept.

VERINO: There you are, all's well that ends well.
She had her obsession fulfilled
and back she came, like Lazarus.
You can't give herbs to the lovesick.
Ovid knew that centuries ago.
So the only possible cure
was the remedy I prescribed.
Give her a week; you won't know her.

SANCHO: Can you do anything for Laida?

VERINO: One thing at a time, good Sancho.
Let's not go rushing our fences.
It's time I had a look at Fedra.

SANCHO: I've sent for her to be brought down.
In fact, that's her coming now.

Scene 10

Enter PISANO and FEDRA.

PISANO: Go in and stand quietly there
or else they'll think you've changed your mind.

FEDRA: Orlando? Isn't he coming?
Orlando? Where is he?

SANCHO: Calm down.
He'll be here in just a minute.

FEDRA: And we'll get married when he comes?

SANCHO: Once the priest comes, as sure as day.

PISANO: I've invited a special guest.
　　He's made a handsome donation.

VERINO: Good, good, the more the merrier.

FEDRA: Let everyone share my joy today.

　　Exit PISANO.

SANCHO: Now Fedra, take this calmly please.

FEDRA: I can't be sane without my madman.

SANCHO: But you will be... after you're married?

FEDRA: Yes, yes, a thousand times over.
　　This has been a squall at sea,
　　a sudden storm that began to rage
　　and no less quickly died away
　　when my ship came in to harbour
　　with its rigging down and its sails torn.

VERINO: We'll get the wind back in your sails.
　　Godspeed, Fedra, Godspeed!

FEDRA:　　　　　　　　　　　　　Orlando!
　　Orlando! Why don't you bring him now?

Scene 11

PISANO ushers in the GENTLEMAN.

GENTLEMAN: With your permission, my good sirs,
　　I've come to witness this wedding feast.

SANCHO: Your company does us honour.

FEDRA: Will Your Honour keep us company?

SANCHO: Pisano, go and get the... hmm... guests,
　　those of them that are... presentable.

What's a wedding without its guests!

Exit PISANO.

FEDRA: Never was truer word spoken!
　　Send out four messengers at once
　　to all the corners of the realm
　　and tell the people of this land
　　that Orlando is wed today,
　　and let there be celebrations
　　from Gibraltar to the Pyrenees.

PISANO returns with some inmates, dragging benches.

PISANO: Some benches.

SANCHO:　　　　　　　　Please, sir, be seated.

GENTLEMAN: Thank you.

FEDRA: Are you going to leave me standing?

VERINO: It's time to bring the bridegroom down.

PISANO: I'll go.

Exit PISANO.

FEDRA:　　　　　　　I'm waiting... and my head hurts...

SANCHO: You give me your word you'll stop this,
　　you'll control your reckless senses,
　　once and for all when you're married?

FEDRA: Then I'll be as sane as you are.
　　But I warn you: if this is a trick...

SANCHO: I would not try and trick my niece.
　　You'd be mad even to think it.

VERINO: (*Aside.*) Careful now. Remember, she is.
　　Raving mad.

FEDRA:　　　　Then where's the best man?

VERINO: It can be one of the inmates.

GENTLEMAN: For such a wonderful wedding;
    I wouldn't dream of such a thing.
    Perhaps I...

VERINO: You are kindness itself.

GENTLEMAN: That's it settled then; I'm best man.

FEDRA: To be best man you must be a knight.

GENTLEMAN: I am a prince of Old Castile.

VERINO: (*Aside to SANCHO.*) I thought I recognised the type.
    Mark my words: there's trouble brewing here.
    Classic case: delusions of grandeur.

SANCHO: (*Aside to VERINO.*) Let's face one problem at a time.

FEDRA: Here he comes, here comes Orlando!

SANCHO: At last! Let the wedding begin!

Scene 12

The inmates appear two by two: THOMAS, MARTIN, BELARDO, LAIDA, MORDACHO, followed by PISANO who is leading FLORIANO by the hand. FLORIANO is dressed as a bridegroom, but in an exaggerated way.

SANCHO: I'd like Fedra next to the groom.
    Laida, you can be bridesmaid.

LAIDA: If I were the last woman on earth,
    I wouldn't do bridesmaid for her.

VERINO: Stay there!

LAIDA: Over my dead body!

SANCHO: All right, let someone else do it.

FEDRA: Such a sensitive little soul.

FLORIANO: Enough arguing for one day!
  Have you no respect for your husband?

FEDRA: Do I not have any rights here?

FLORIANO: You can't have any rights. You're mad.
  Or had you forgotten?

FEDRA: Hardly.

FLORIANO: So not another word from you
  until it's time to say 'I do'.

FEDRA: Who do you think you're talking to?

BELARDO: The soul ages with arguments.

FLORIANO: I'm talking to my future wife.
  Or have you suddenly changed your mind?

SANCHO: That's enough! A mild contretemps,
  a tiff between two starred lovers.

FLORIANO: It would be best to say nothing
  for the truth here would cut like a knife.

FEDRA: There are things that I could say too!

SANCHO: All right! All right!

MORDACHO: We're hanging about
  like spare parts. We look like half-wits.

THOMAS: I don't think much of this wedding.

MARTIN: I feel a chapter coming on.

LAIDA: Fedra was always a lying bitch.
  In her wedding dress she looks like a witch.

SANCHO: Doctor, this is getting out of hand.

VERINO: Belardo, some entertainment.
  Get them to dance.

BELARDO: Have I a choice,
but to organise this danse macabre?

The inmates dance a masque and then, with the exception of
LAIDA, all of them leave.

Scene 13

Enter VALERIO and ERIFILA.

VALERIO: Why are you doing this to me?

ERIFILA: It's not you that I'm running from;
it's my life I'm running towards.

SANCHO: What's going on here?

VALERIO: This madwoman,
as soon as she set foot in my house,
howled as though the floor were molten,
picked up her skirts and came running here.
I followed her as best I could.

SANCHO: What's this all about, Elvira?
Why treat this good man so cruelly?
He only wants the best for you.

ERIFILA: His was a house full of sadness;
all my happiness, all my joy
were here, in this place of madness.
I'd have died if I'd stayed away.

VALERIO: There's neither rhyme nor reason to this.

ERIFILA: Who's looking for rhyme or reason?
This is madness, this is passion.
This is beyond the peace of love
and there is no greater affliction
in this world than jealousy.
Give up all hope for me,
for all I want is Orlando.

VALERIO: Orlando is out of his mind,

we all know that. Leave her to me.
Who knows what evil influence
he has exercised on her poor brain.

FLORIANO: My friend, there's no sense to what you say.
If she's acting without reason,
as you claim, I cannot be blamed.
If she's mad, then no one's to blame.

ERIFILA: Are you married?

FLORIANO: Yes, I'm married.
Can't you see all the guests are here?

ERIFILA: You mean you actually did it?
You bastard! Treacherous bastard!

FLORIANO: I married her because you left,
because you said you hated me,
because you loved Valerio,
or have you lost your memory
as well as your mind? You left me,
and in front of these witnesses
I command you to go back home.
Blood flows much thicker than water;
don't disappoint your loving cousin.

ERIFILA: I didn't believe you would do it.

FLORIANO: (*Aside.*) She really thinks I married her.

ERIFILA: If you think I'll lie down and die
or turn silently to the wall,
that I'll let her take you away,
then you'd do well to think again.

FLORIANO: (*Aside.*) God knows what she's likely to say...

ERIFILA: Because, Floriano, if you think
murder can hide behind madness...

FLORIANO: (*Aside.*) God! She's killed me by her own hand.

(*Aloud.*) Ha! Ha! Ha!

ERIFILA: That you can hide here
after the greatest crime of all,
the murder of Prince Reinero.

SANCHO: Reinero... Floriano... you!

FLORIANO: Ha! Her brains have finally addled.
(*Aside.*) I'm dead.

SANCHO: Seize him.

FLORIANO: I'm mad, insane.
How could I have killed anyone?

PISANO: You're as sane as anyone here!

SANCHO: Seize him. There'll be a rich reward.
Valerio, I blame you for this.

VALERIO: He was my friend, what was I to do?

GENTLEMAN: Have I got the right end of the stick?
You say this man killed Reinero?
If that's all he did, let him go.

VERINO: Ah, I knew it!

SANCHO: You must be mad!
Who do you think you are, butting...

GENTLEMAN: Tell them if I'm mad, Orlando.

FLORIANO: You're a ghost that's sent to haunt me!

GENTLEMAN: Touch my hand.

FLORIANO: Your Highness, Prince Rei...
I don't understand. I killed you.

VALERIO: You're Reinero?

GENTLEMAN: At your service, sir.

VALERIO: This is some sort of mad charade,

something dreamt up for carnival.

GENTLEMAN: I can assure you; I'm Reinero.

VERINO: Floriano didn't kill you then.

GENTLEMAN: I see you are a logician, sir.
My death was engineered. A ruse.

FLORIANO: A ruse! What sort of ruse was that?

GENTLEMAN: You and I loved the same woman:
Celia, the flower and the star
of the town of Zaragoza.
I was desperate to win her heart.
I held fiestas outside her house,
tournaments with brave and noble knights,
colourful dances and music,
bullfights, parades and processions;
and I would send her emerald rings,
bracelets of the finest amethyst,
all engraved with secret messages,
with codes and cyphers and symbols
that I hoped her heart would understand.
But nothing... no, worse than nothing.
She seemed to hold me in disdain.
One dark night I went to her house,
pulled there like a moth to the light,
accompanied by three of my men.
One of them a page, dressed like me,
looking like me in every way
was to wait outside in the street.
It was a simple and easy trick
to keep my name from prying eyes.
It was that page you wounded
and who later died there, in the street.
I ordered my men to silence
and had my untimely death announced.
By noon the news spread far and wide;
the whole city was moved to tears,
and I sent spies to Celia's house

to report to me her reaction.
The page was buried that afternoon
with all the pomp due to a prince.
I rode south to Valencia,
a city that I've always loved.
A messenger arrived today;
Celia's beside herself with grief.
He lovely face is stained with tears
and she's locked herself away.
I leave Valencia tomorrow
and would be glad to take you with me.
We'd make good travelling companions,
you the madman and me the corpse.

FLORIANO: The sky has opened up for me!

VERINO: Let me say I am delighted
to have my diagnosis confirmed.
I have always said: 'Here's a sane man.'
And by God, you're as sane as I.

SANCHO: What happens now to Elvira?

VERINO: A more tragic case altogether.
Her madness is beyond repair.

ERIFILA: My name is not Elvira.

VERINO: No?
(*Aside to SANCHO.*) This is an attack coming on.

FLORIANO: Her real name is Erifila,
she was robbed by her servant
and she's as sane as you or I.

VERINO: You have no grounds for that statement.
Now my considered judgement,
based on my study of Galen...

SANCHO: Erifila, you must forgive us.

VALERIO: (*To FLORIANO.*) It's you Erifila loves, my
friend,

and there's not a force on this earth
that should ever come between you.
Marry her, and with my blessing.

FLORIANO: You've given me the gift of life
twice over, my friend Valerio.
Erifila?

ERIFILA: Floriano,
give my regards to your good wife.

FLORIANO: It was a piece of theatre, a sham.
I told you that; for Fedra's sake.

ERIFILA: You've sailed close to the wind, my love
But this time I shall forgive you
Just this once.

FEDRA: And what about me?

GENTLEMAN: Is there anyone who will take
our jilted bride?

VALERIO: If she were sane...
I confess I find her pretty...
But not another madwoman.
I need love. I yearn for quiet,
not constant fits and bursts of fury.

FEDRA: My madness was merely pretence,
a trick to win Orlando's heart.

LAIDA: (*Aside.*) Ah, into his heart... not his bed.

SANCHO: You're not mad?

FEDRA: Not in the slightest,
dear uncle, dear doctor, dear friends.
Valerio, I will be your wife.

VALERIO: And I'm the happiest of men.

LAIDA: You all think I'm mad too, don't you?

SANCHO: Is there any reason to think not?

LAIDA: There's every reason... lots of them.

VERINO: I've diagnosed you already.
A classic case of melancholia.

LAIDA: Fedra simply imitated me.
I'd be happy now to be a maid,
to go back to what I was before.
I'd be happy scrubbing and washing.
Please don't lock me up again... please.

GENTLEMAN: Is there anyone in this madhouse
who is mad?

They look towards VERINO.

VERINO: (*Referring to LAIDA.*) Melancholia.
The surging of the black humours
under the baleful sign of Saturn.

GENTLEMAN: So let the marriages take place
with the greatest celebration.

VALERIO: Though surely not in this bleak place.

GENTLEMAN: And then we ride for Zaragoza.

*They all leave, except LAIDA, a lonely figure looking for lost pebbles.
A heavy door slams shut behind the departing guests.*

End of Act Three.

EPILOGUE

BELARDO: This is not the way things should be,
  loose ends and jagged shards of words.
  Art is harmony as life is,
  and Laida should not be left thus.
  Was her wrong-doing any greater?
  Let us see things a different way:
  When he flees from Erifila
  Leonato meets the Gentleman
  and enters upon his service.
  A coincidence, but possible.
  The curious wedding's announced
  and Leonato attends it too.
  More than that, he becomes best man
  though we can imagine his fear
  as Erifila re-appears
  like a ghost from his sordid past.
  But then he hears Verino speak:
  'A more tragic case altogether.
  Her madness is beyond repair',
  His former mistress has gone mad
  in the words of a learned doctor.
  His jellied guts turn into valour:

  So perhaps.

VERINO: A more tragic case altogether.
  Her madness is beyond repair.

LEONATO: I think I should say something here.
  I'm prepared to be her husband,
  although I was her servant once.
  Madwomen cannot be choosers.

SANCHO: You know her. Then enlighten us.

LEONATO: I rescued her from cruel parents
　　　and led her to this paradise.
　　　I looked after her day and night,
　　　I respected her chaste honour.

ERIFILA: You chased my honour night in, night out;
　　　then you stripped me and stole my jewels!

VERINO: The obsessive melancholic.
　　　The surging of the black humours
　　　under the baleful sign of Saturn.

GENTLEMAN: You'd do well to tell the truth, boy.

LEONATO: I've still got them. She can have them back.

SANCHO: In that case they can be married!

FLORIANO: Erifila, for that's her real name,
　　　has been promised to Valerio.
　　　And I owe Valerio my life.

VALERIO: (*To FLORIANO.*) It's you Erifila loves, my friend,
　　　and there's not a force on this earth
　　　that should ever come between you.
　　　Marry her, and with my blessing.

FLORIANO: You've given me the gift of life
　　　twice over, my friend Valerio.
　　　Erifila?

ERIFILA: Floriano,
　　　give my regards to your good wife.

FLORIANO: It was a piece of theatre, a sham.
　　　I told you that; for Fedra's sake.

ERIFILA: Then, my love, I shall forgive you.
　　　Just this once.

FEDRA:　　　　　　And what about me?

GENTLEMAN: Is there anyone who will take

our jilted bride?

VALERIO: If she were sane...
 I confess I find her pretty...
 But not another madwoman.
 I need love. I yearn for quiet,
 not constant fits and bursts of fury.

FEDRA: My madness was merely pretence,
 a trick to win Orlando's heart.

LAIDA: (*Aside.*) Ah, into his heart... not his bed.

SANCHO: You're not mad?

FEDRA: Not in the slightest,
 dear uncle, dear doctor, dear friends.
 Valerio, I will be your wife.

VALERIO: And I'm the happiest of men.

LAIDA: You all think I'm mad too, don't you?

SANCHO: Is there any reason to think not?

LAIDA: There's every reason... lots of them.

VERINO: I've diagnosed you already.
 A classic case of melancholia.

LAIDA: Fedra simply imitated me.
 I'd be happy now to be a maid,
 to go back to what I was before.
 I'd be happy scrubbing and washing.
 Please don't lock me up again... please.

GENTLEMAN: Is there anyone in this madhouse
 who is really mad? Listen, boy,
 here's your chance to make restitution.

LEONATO: Sir, I need no second bidding,
 for this maid to be mine. Sweet Laida,

you and I are kindred spirits,
and I see in your soul a beauty
matched only by your lovely face.
Do you think you could care for me?

LAIDA: Sir, you give me life and freedom,
and I shall worship your every step.

GENTLEMAN: So let the marriages take place
with the greatest celebration.
Then we ride for Zaragoza.

FLORIANO: The man who murdered you breathes again
and thanks you for his life renewed.

The End.

PERIBAÑEZ AND THE COMENDADOR OF OCAÑA

Thanks to Dominic Dromgoole and Dr Melveena McKendrick for help with this version; the cast of the first production for their spirit and skill; the Marlowe Society and Tim Cribb for commissioning and supporting the project; and the National Theatre Studio for workshops on early drafts of this version directed by Simon Usher.

Preface

In 1983 I went to live in Spain, in the Alpujarras mountains between Granada and the sea. I found myself in an old, rural world of stone threshing circles, implements and clothes, crops and harvests, local comedians and tragedians. The town had a hundred bars and one bus stop. Gypsies lived under the bridge. During the insane summer fiesta, the statue of the Virgin was paraded through the streets while homemade high-explosive fireworks were detonated; children threw fire-crackers at the feet of the dancers.

So when I came across *Peribañez*, some years later, I felt an instant connection with its world. I also thought it was a wonderful play which had not, to my knowledge, had a full production in English. The first scene is a marvellous celebratory shout of love. Peribañez, tormented by jealousy, undergoes a trial of inner and outer ennoblement. Comedy and tragedy, lust and love, purity and danger, ambition and honour are explored dramatically through bladed ambivalences, a pacy story, and vivid dramatic poetry. Rustic comedy and lovely songs are juxtaposed with impassioned arias and tragic soliloquies. Above all the writing has a sense of exceptional poetic energy. All of this is a challenge to the translator.

I have deliberately called this a *version*, rather than a translation. Since translation is never a transparent act – a simple transfer of meanings, qualities and details from one language into another – the process, for all its endeavour at precise faithfulness, is inevitably one of change and alteration. This has to do with the endless particulars and variables of the languages; different emphases, different verbal music, different contexts, different implications, the different worlds of the different languages. I have tried to make a version of *Peribañez* which has fidelity to the original *and* which will play in a way that satisfies me, in the English-speaking theatre now.

While most of the version is as faithful as I have been able to make it, I'd like to mention some of the liberties I have taken. Firstly, I have not tried to mimic Lope's various intricate verse-forms – redondillas, octavos reales, romances, etc. English is not nearly as rich as Spanish in rhyme or assonance, and I didn't want a rhyming straightjacket or a detailed reproduction at the expense of sense and strength. I decided the best choice, and the nearest equivalent to Lope, was a variable octosyllabic line which, although potentially capable of the requisite intricacy and balance and rhetorical gravity at points, could also be fast, free and playable in English. It also avoids the perils of Shakespearean pastiche inherent in blank verse – which also carries for an English audience expectations which Lope's plays confound.

I wanted to avoid untranslatable references and archaisms, translationese and literalness in the worst sense: so certain passages have been shortened (such as Leonardo's speech in Act 3 Scene 2, and the King's dialogue in Act 3 Scene 7) because the joke wore thin in English. I have freely adapted a few other passages, notably Peribañez's soliloquy in Act 3 Scene 4; this speech must dramatise Peribañez at breaking point; the impending violence is palpable, he's heading inexorably towards the crisis point. He's in a kind of lucid trance; he's just ridden back by night, he knows he has to kill the Comendador. I decided to keep the original's paean of praise to his horse to one line, and to transfer the puns of the Spanish (caña, Ocaña) into an image of a harvested field of cane lit by the monochromatic light-bulb of the moon.

Lope's use of songs is wonderful. They are intrinsic to the play as dramatic irony, or as a key moment of celebratory expression, or as – in the case of the Harvester's song – both an essential plot clue for Peribañez, and a way of making the story hesitate, slowing the progress of Peribañez's resolution. I have freely adapted the song lyrics, and to an extent the 'A-Z of love' speeches in Act 1 Scene 1 – because they work better in English this way, while I hope sustaining the play of meanings and the tone of the Spanish.

The comedy was in some ways the hardest thing to do. There's a real danger that what was funny in 1612 will seem ludicrous to an audience in 1998. So, in Lope's own spirit of improvisation, and as an attempt to recreate the intrinsic humour rather than keeping it faithful to the exact word, the meeting of the four villagers in Act 2 Scene 1 and the Harvesters' scene in Act 3 are slightly expanded in my version, and the tone departs from the comic-pastoral literary aesthetic.

Perhaps the most heretical thing I've done is add some emphases to the last scenes of Act 3. These additions seemed to worked well in the Cambridge Arts Theatre production. Although the last act of *Peribañez* shifts gear, it also seems to me at key points too abbreviated, too rushed, as if the conventions of the genre threatened to overtake the natural shape of the action and limit the scope of its resolution. So I briefly developed some of the exchanges in Scene 6 between Casilda, Ines and the Comendador. I gave the Comendador a slightly longer speech, and Ines a longer speech of self-justification. Peribañez's speech as he stands listening in the dark to the Comendador and his wife also seemed to need more cruxes, more sense of the breaking point being reached.

The last scene was especially difficult. As I understand it, it seems to affirm the King's authority and at the same time to set against the pomp an undertone of irony. The dialogue between the King and Queen has an acidic edge to it; a tense and odd subtext. The courtly flattery carries an opposing twist. Likewise the King's self-made and self-styled claim to justice is simultaneously made doubtful as he fails (until hastily reminded by the Queen) to allow Peribañez the right to defend himself.

The very last moment of the play – in which Peribañez wraps up the proceedings on a conventional note – also seemed abrupt and inadequate to the huge arc the central characters have travelled. And Casilda has been lost altogether – hardly a single line since the death of the Comendador. Yet she is the one who can best sum up their relationship at the end – based not on the ambitious desire for upward social mobility, but on a deep (and costly) sense of where true love lies. So I have added a brief epilogue which gives her the last word she seems so richly to deserve.

Nick Drake
London, 1998

Characters

PERIBAÑEZ

CASILDA

PRIEST, uncle to Casilda

INES, cousin to Casilda

COSTANZA

BARTOLO

COMENDADOR

LUJAN, servant to the Comendador

MARIN, servant to the Comendador

SANCHO

LEONARDO, manservant to the Comendador

KING ENRIQUE

CONSTABLE

ARTIST

BLAS, a villager

GIL, a villager

ANTON, a villager

BENITO, a villager

MENDO, a harvester

LLORENTE, a harvester

CHAPARRO, a harvester

HELIPE, a harvester

GOMEZ

QUEEN

3 COUNCILLORS

PAGE

SERVANT

MUSICIANS

LADIES IN WAITING

PERIBAÑEZ AND THE COMENDADOR OF OCAÑA
was first performed at the Cambridge Arts Theatre on the 11th
of March 1997 with the following cast:

PERIBAÑEZ, Ed Waters
CASILDA, Naomie Harris
PRIEST, ARTIST, GOMEZ, Eliot Shrimpton
INES, Madeleine Worrall
COSTANZA, Hannah Dawson
BARTOLO, Robbie Hudson
COMENDADOR, Rufus Jones
LUJAN, Patrick Nielsen
MARIN, IST COUNCILLOR, David Smith
SANCHO, Kate-Olivia Higginbottom
LEONARDO, Scott Brooksbank
KING ENRIQUE, Duncan Parrish
CONSTABLE, Stefan Naylor
BLAS, Richard Jones
GIL, David Pinson
ANTON, Chris Moran
BENITO, Phil Lane
MENDO, Ian Bartram
LLORENTE, Rebecca Johnson
HELIPE, Naomi Benson
QUEEN, SERVANT,
MENGA, BLAS, Hannah Roberts
2ND COUNCILLOR, Michael Chance
3RD COUNCILLOR, Jeremy Cosgrove

Directors: Dominic Dromgoole, Angus Jackson
Assistant director: Simon Godwin

ACT ONE

Scene 1

Early August, 1406. Heat. Whitewashed walls. Midday's strong bright light. Then –

Enter a wedding party, including the PRIEST, INES the bridesmaid, COSTANZA, CASILDA the bride and PERIBAÑEZ the groom. Shouts of celebration.

INES: I wish you years and years of joy.

COSTANZA: And I hope you'll both be the immortals of
happiness.

CASILDA: I'll never live up to all this joy,
all this honour, all your good wishes.
I wish the same for both of you:
good men and a happy marriage.

PRIEST: All your good wishing and hoping
is very kind and courteous:
but it's also superficial chatter;
nothing you say can ever match
the grace of God's best wishes.
All happiness depends on Him;
and let that be the final word.

INES: I simply wish them happiness.

PRIEST: I know you do. And so do I.
God helps good folk. And besides,
my niece is very sensible.

PERIBAÑEZ: I know she is. She proves it by
her simple lack of jealousy.

CASILDA: Jealousy? Never give me cause
to feel that monster in my heart.

PERIBAÑEZ: I promise you I never will.

INES: They say the gods made jealousy
    as the price we pay for love.

PRIEST: Enough! Enough! Sit down and eat –
    the food looks good! Let's celebrate
    the day these two are joined as one.

PERIBAÑEZ makes a speech to the GUESTS.

PERIBAÑEZ: Thank you all for being here
    together on this special day.
    I'm a married man – I'm a better man –
    and it feels wonderful! My friends,
    this woman makes me what I am;
    she brings me hope and happiness.
    Please raise your glasses in a toast
    to the beauty God has given me.

They toast the bride.

PRIEST: Quite right God takes the credit.
    She's the loveliest girl in the town,
    indeed in the whole province
    for all I know. Her beauty proves
    the miracle of Creation –

CASILDA: Husband, I love you more than enough
    to pay you back in full and in kind
    for all your fine and tender words.
    But if I do you owe me back
    equally as much again.

PERIBAÑEZ: Casilda, it is impossible
    you love me more than I love you;
    the debt cannot be paid in talk,
    so do not even try. Listen:
    I'd lay this town before your feet,
    with all the richest fields that lie
    along the glittering river, as far

as the ocean's blue horizon.
An olive tree's rich cargo
and a meadow of spring flowers at dawn
are less beautiful than you.
The first red apple in the hand
and the first-pressed oil from the mill
glimmering gold in the jar
mean less to me than you.
Even a chilled and pure white wine
in a crystal glass would taste less fine,
less perfect than your lips.
You see: we farmers love good wine
as lords love their red roses.
I love December, for grafting,
and October's golden ripeness,
and the quiet rains in May,
and unwinnowed corn in August;
but I love you more than all these things
that make the paradise we share
now that our wedding day is here.
My heart's desire, live in me
and by divine and human right
we will be the King and Queen
of our peaceful kingdom
and everyone will say: Casilda
is a beautiful *and* happy wife.

CASILDA: Husband: how can I describe
        the little things I see in you,
        when to me they mean so much,
        here in my heart? I never heard
        a song that set me dancing
        and whirling like a swallow
        as you do each time I see you.
        Even on Midsummer's Day
        at dawn when all my friends cry out,
        shouting and laughing across the fields,
        I never felt such joy as when

I hear your voice calling my name.
Even the tuned strings of a guitar,
its perfect curves and steady neck,
can't play the music of our love.
Dancing feet in shining shoes
aren't as excited as my heart.
You stand out from a crowd of men;
you're wild as a young bull in spring,
you're fresher than a new white shirt,
you're the tallest Easter candle,
the sweetest holy bread.
But in the end I love you
for yourself, just as you are.

A long kiss. Applause.

PRIEST: That's enough love-talk and kissing.
The musicians are ready to play.

PERIBAÑEZ: I'm sorry; you must have heard
all this a thousand times before.
To you it's old. To us it's new.
Now: let there be music and dancing.

The MUSICIANS play and PEOPLE dance.

Bless the bride
This May morning;
Streams run clear,
Green alders raise
New green buds
Almond blossom
Strews the way,
And the young grass
Full of dew
Guards the lily
Pure and true

*Love's new morning
With God's blessing*

Man and Woman
Joined as one

From the height
Of icy mountains
Through the ancient
Oaks and pines
Let the flowing
Waters pass
To the valleys
Where the nightingales
Hidden in
The secret leaves
Sing of love

Love's new morning
With God's blessing
Man and Woman
Joined as one

The music is interrupted by a commotion and shouts offstage.

Enter BARTOLO.

BARTOLO: They've brought three wild young bulls
    into the plaza; one's a real Spaniard –
    it took an hour just to rope him.
    Young Blas was tossed twice through the air
    like an acrobat; I've never seen
    anyone move so fast. Tomas
    lost his trousers, so now we've seen
    the proof he's just a little boy –
    no wonder he still can't grow a beard.
    And then the young Comendador
    dressed in all his finest clothes,
    as swift and silent as a hawk
    decides to have a go at him.
    I swear to God, if the bull had been loose –

PRIEST: Dear Lord, don't let it come near me.
    I'm terrified of animals.
    I live in fear of my own cat.

BARTOLO: It's heading straight this way now, fast.

PRIEST: Then I'm retreating, I'm not proud.
    Each man for himself; where can I hide?

COSTANZA: Don't be afraid; recite it a prayer.

PRIEST: Prayer's useless at a time like this.

COSTANZA: You'd puzzle and confuse the beast,
    and then he might forget to charge.

INES: Or you might perform a miracle
    and change him into an angel.

PRIEST: You forget: bulls don't speak Latin.

He exits. More voices.

INES: Let's all go out to see it.

COSTANZA: There's no danger if it's tied up.

BARTOLO: It's tethered on a short sharp rope,
    but it's still mad and dangerous.
    I want to see who'll take him on.

PERIBAÑEZ: (*To CASILDA.*) What do you think; should I
                                                            chance it?

CASILDA: No: it's far too dangerous.

PERIBAÑEZ: Even if it's twice as terrifying
    as everyone says, for you my love
    I'll grasp the horns and force it
    to bow down on its knees to me,
    and show them all how strong I am.

CASILDA: My love, you should not be the one
    to grasp a horn of any sort
    today of all days. Stay with me.

They kiss.

Then more noise and commotion.

CASILDA: Something's wrong –

More shouts.

Enter BARTOLO.

BARTOLO: Bad news on your wedding day;
   they should have left the bull in peace;
   those idiots should be ashamed.
   But as for the animal, I curse it:
   may it be fed dead roadside stalks,
   and stay locked up in its dark stall,
   frustrated, charging four close walls
   when it's on heat, and may the streams
   run dry when it's parched with summer thirst.
   May it be slaughtered clumsily
   in a backstreet, and never see
   the inside of a bull-ring
   and a decently heroic death.
   May some unskilled commoner
   butcher it and spatter its blood
   on street sweepings and dust.

PERIBAÑEZ: You sound like a ranting actor.
   Calm down. Tell us: what has happened?

BARTOLO: Our noble Lord Comendador,
   reigning his bay mare so hard
   the silver bit was white with foam,
   as I said before, was riding past
   and saw the bull let loose; and so
   decided to have a go at him.
   First he took off his scarlet cloak,
   set his hat at an angle,
   freed his sword-arm and weapon,
   and crouched down in the saddle;
   then suddenly he spurred the horse,
   which sprang forward through the air
   dividing the crowd before him. But then
   the rope tangled the horse, which stumbled,

fell, and threw the Comendador
down among the crowd. He hit his head
bang! on the ground. He might be dead.
They're bringing him here now.

*The unconscious COMENDADOR is brought in by several
VILLAGERS, his two footmen/grooms, MARIN and LUJAN,
and SANCHO. They are wearing riding/hunting clothes.*

LUJAN: Quickly, get him a chair.

MARIN: Someone fetch the doctor. Run!

SANCHO: The Priest can give him the last rites.

INES: I think he fled upstairs to hide.

PERIBAÑEZ: Go and find him, Bartolo.

BARTOLO exits.

LUJAN: We should be prepared for the worst.
How are we going to carry him home?

MARIN: Do you think he's dead?

LUJAN: No sign of life.

MARIN and LUJAN exit.

CASILDA: He's still breathing. Pedro, quickly
bring me a glass of water.

PERIBAÑEZ: If the Comendador dies in our house
on our wedding day, I swear
I'll curse this day and leave this place.

*Everyone exits, leaving CASILDA with the COMENDA-
DOR. He is unconscious in a chair. She is warming his hands.*

CASILDA: Comendador, you must not die;
if you can hear me, listen;
you are a famous knight, my Lord;
your sword strikes the terror of death

into the enemy; the whole world knows
you have killed hundreds in battle,
braved fear and fate, and lived;
so how can an ordinary rope
trip and bring you down like this;
you, our Lord Comendador?
Please don't blight my wedding day
and the hopes of my marriage.
Perhaps you don't remember me,
but I have often seen you pass
through the village in your glory,
in your fine clothes and jewellery.
I could never speak to you.
Now listen to me. My Lord?
Comendador? Can you hear me?

The COMENDADOR comes back to life. He sees CASILDA
in her wedding dress.

COMENDADOR: Where am I? Who are you?

CASILDA: This is a house in the village.
You had an accident. You are safe.
You are welcome here.

COMENDADOR: I remember falling to the ground.
Then I opened my eyes and saw myself
from high in the air. Everything
was very clear and still.
I thought I was in Heaven.
Perhaps I am.
Don't disillusion me;
don't let me fall to earth again;
are you an angel?

CASILDA: You must still be close to death.

COMENDADOR: Why so?

CASILDA: Because you are seeing visions.
Sir, this may be gratitude

for returning to life in this room
in my house. But it's only for today.

COMENDADOR: So you must be the happy bride?

CASILDA: Unhappy, if this is my fault
and you grow worse, not better.

COMENDADOR: You're married, then.

CASILDA: Married and happy.

COMENDADOR: Both at the same time?
Few lovely women are so lucky.

CASILDA: Then I've had the plain girls' luck.

COMENDADOR: (*Aside.*) How can such a beauty
be married to a peasant?

(*To CASILDA.*) What is your name?

CASILDA: My name is Casilda, Sir.

COMENDADOR: (*Aside.*) She halts my heart.
She's like a diamond set in lead.

(*To CASILDA.*) The lucky man who married you
must be... extremely happy.

CASILDA: Oh no, Sir: I'm the lucky one.

COMENDADOR: You have all the grace and beauty
to marry a nobleman, like me.
Allow me to offer you –

Enter PERIBAÑEZ.

PERIBAÑEZ: The Priest has vanished. If he dies –

CASILDA: Stop. He is himself again.
Lord Fadrique has recovered.

PERIBAÑEZ: So I see.
That is good news.

Congratulations, my love.
You are welcome here, my Lord.

COMENDADOR: Such was the heavenly power
of this angel and her healing touch;
she has brought me back to life.

Enter MARIN and LUJAN.

MARIN: He's awake. Can you walk, Sir?

LUJAN: We brought the old carriage
to carry you home.

COMENDADOR: As you can see
that won't be necessary.

LUJAN: Thank God for your recovery!

COMENDADOR: (*To PERIBAÑEZ and CASILDA.*)
If I thank anyone it should be you;
the debt I owe will be repaid
as soon as I am recovered.

PERIBAÑEZ: I would offer you my own good health
if that would help –

COMENDADOR: I believe you. But it's not required.

LUJAN: How are you feeling, Sir?

COMENDADOR: I am in agony; I suffer
a new and terrible desire.

LUJAN: I don't quite understand.

COMENDADOR: That does not matter.

LUJAN: I was referring to your fall.

COMENDADOR: And so was I; when I opened my eyes
darkness fell; and now my life
and everything I have achieved
could be destroyed by one mad thought.

They exit, leaving CASILDA and PERIBAÑEZ alone.

PERIBAÑEZ: So. He seems quite well again.

What happened?

CASILDA: The shock of it –

PERIBAÑEZ: A bad omen on our wedding day.

CASILDA: Perhaps it's not so serious.
He recovered quickly from the fall.
I talked to him, then he woke up;
he spoke to me, and now he's gone.
If we need anything from him
perhaps he'll help us in return.

PERIBAÑEZ: Yes, you've earned his favour.
And here we are, alone at last
in our own house. Everyone's gone,
the party's over, and the time has come
for my love's satisfaction.
You are the mistress of this house,
as you know, according to God
a good wife always obeys her man;
do not forget Adam and Eve
and we'll have peace and happiness.
You'll turn my sorrows into joy.

CASILDA: So tell me what makes a good wife?
In your opinion?

PERIBAÑEZ: I will.

CASILDA: I'm listening.

PERIBAÑEZ: According to the alphabet of love:
A is for Adoration,
B is for Beauty,
C is for Carefulness,
D is for Discretion,
E is for Enchantment,

F is for Faithfulness,
G is for Goodness,
H is for Honour,
I is for being Idolised,
J is for Jubilation,
K is for Kindness, L for Love,
M is for the Miracle of Marriage,
N is for saying No when Necessary,
O is the other letter in No,
P is for Passion and Peace,
Q is for Quietness, R is Rejoicing,
S is for Serenity,
T is for Tenderness and Truth
U is for Understanding,
V is for Virtue and Variety,
W is for Wisdom and Wonder,
X is for Extraordinary,
Y is for Yearning,
and Z is for love's Zodiac.
Learn this alphabet and be
the glorious flower of this town;
I'll be its foremost nobleman.

CASILDA: I'll study your alphabet carefully;
but since now I've heard yours, my love,
may I recite one just for you?

PERIBAÑEZ: Please do; I want to learn from you.

CASILDA: Sit still and listen patiently:
A: do not be Arrogant;
B: be the Best Bridegroom;
C: be my Constant Companion;
D: be Devoted only to me;
E: be Elegant but Easy,
F: be Faithful, G: Gallant;
H is Hope and Honesty,
I is for Illumination,
J for Joy, K: Kiss me Quick;

L is simple – Love for Life.
M is for Magnificent Man,
N is Never Neglect my Needs,
O is Only, Only, Only –
P is for Protection, Q
is Quickness and Quiver;
R is for Revelation,
S is for this Song of Songs;
T is Touch, U is United,
V is Virgin, W is Warm,
X is Kisses in our bed,
Y is Yes, and Yes, and Yes:
and Z is the Zephyr of your snores...

Pause. They embrace and kiss.

PERIBAÑEZ: We'll learn these alphabets by heart.
What else have we to give but love?

CASILDA: Then perhaps today of all days,
the first of our new life together,
I should not ask for a favour.

PERIBAÑEZ: I would grant you anything.

CASILDA: Are you sure?

PERIBAÑEZ: Your wish is my command. Now wish
and I will make your dreams come true.

CASILDA: The Fiesta of the Assumption
is next week in Toledo.
My greatest wish in all the world
is to visit the Shrine of the Virgin
then see her grand procession
when the King and all his noblemen
follow her through the crowded streets
all through the day and night.

PERIBAÑEZ: Your wish is granted, my Lady.

CASILDA: You're W for Wonderful, good Sir.

PERIBAÑEZ: Let's invite your cousins,
    and travel together in style.
    And when we're there I'll buy you –

CASILDA: Yes?

PERIBAÑEZ: – something to wear, expensive and soft,
    which when we're alone you can slip off.

    Exit.

Scene 2

The COMENDADOR's house in Ocaña. Later that afternoon. Enter the COMENDADOR and LEONARDO, his manservant.

COMENDADOR: Leonardo, get Lujan. Now!

LEONARDO: I've called him, Sir.

COMENDADOR: Call him again.

LEONARDO: He's still changing, Sir

COMENDADOR: I want him now!

LEONARDO: (*Aside.*) He's recovered from the blow,
    but he's still crying and sighing;
    anyone would think he's dying.
    I've heard those moans before; he's sick
    with the hopeless misery of love.

    He exits, leaving the COMENDADOR alone.

COMENDADOR: A village beauty; but you are
    as clear and brilliant as the dawn
    discovering the mountain's peaks.
    I dreamed it was spring, and Zephyr
    had breathed and blown upon Flora
    in the rich green of the meadows.
    You were there picking wild flowers;
    I saw you touch them into bloom
    like the new shoots of hope in my heart.

Lucky the man who reaps from your love
a harvest of gold; for such treasure
the Sun would lend his chariot
or Night the Plough of Seven Stars;
and I'd give houses, forts and towns,
gold, and all I am, to hold
what that peasant has in his straw bed.

Enter LUJAN.

COMENDADOR: Why have you kept me waiting?

LUJAN: I was stabling the horses.

COMENDADOR: Lujan, I am a dead man;
    the power of that moment
    still shakes me to the core.

LUJAN: Are you still thinking about that?

COMENDADOR: You stood at my side
    at our victory in Granada;
    I witnessed your honour and bravery;
    I have enjoyed discussing with you
    my most private meditations;
    so let your answer to my question
    reveal the kind of man you are:
    because a thoughtful and discreet
    friend will always earn respect,
    regardless of rank, and would certainly be
    considered for promotion.

LUJAN: I'll help in any way I can;
    you always command my loyalty.

COMENDADOR: If I wanted to make this man,
    this villager, my cordial friend,
    how would I proceed? Perhaps
    some unexpected generosity
    to show my proper gratitude
    for their hospitality?

LUJAN: If – for the sake of example – I
　　was secretly in love with his wife
　　here's what I'd do. Before the woman
　　I'd win the husband over first.
　　Locally, he's much-admired
　　as an honourable man;
　　but some well-chosen gift from you
　　and he'll drop his guard like all the rest;
　　these peasants are out for what they can get.
　　And since you're the Comendador,
　　and he'll owe you a favour after all,
　　he'll sensibly turn a blind eye.

COMENDADOR: I see. What should I give him first?
　　As an initial inducement?
　　Some tools, or a case of wine?
　　Perhaps some field I do not want?

LUJAN: Bearing in mind your noble rank
　　will flatter the peasant anyway,
　　give him two mules; these animals
　　are more valuable to a man like him
　　than the whole of Ocaña –
　　and for his wife, gold earrings perhaps?
　　Remember how in poetry
　　women are always seduced by gifts,
　　while for their sake their true loves
　　die horribly on the battlefield?

COMENDADOR: The poets' words are true –

LUJAN: You may be quite certain, a gift
　　is the way to a wise man's heart.
　　A favour given publicly
　　betrays your love and will not work;
　　but a gift does its work secretly,
　　its feet are shod in silence.

COMENDADOR: Good, then let us give –

LUJAN: Its power bridges the wide oceans,
and brings low the highest mountains!
All shall be well; wait and see.

COMENDADOR: Release me from this misery.

LUJAN: This is the best way.

COMENDADOR: Then you must buy the finest mules
Ocaña will ever have seen.

LUJAN: Yoke them to your plan and see
how quickly time will yield your crop:
for the harvest of love grows tenfold
when seeded with a shower of gold.

They exit.

Scene 3

The village square. Morning. INES, COSTANZA and CASILDA.

INES: Nearly ready?

CASILDA: Yes. I can't wait.
How long does the journey take?

COSTANZA: This time of year about ten hours,
or sometimes less –

INES: The road is good –

CASILDA: And the weather's perfect!
So. What are you going to wear?

INES: A shawl, and what I'm wearing now.

COSTANZA: I'm going in my embroidered dress
with the silver-thread stitched all round here –

She demonstrates around her breasts.

INES: Make sure you open up your shawl
to show off your advantages –

CASILDA: And I'm going in a red wool skirt
   with the proper velvet top –
   a married woman in her best.

COSTANZA: Anton's wife lent me her dress
   made from that lovely Cuenca cloth,
   a deep sky-blue; but Menga said
   'it doesn't go with your colouring.'

INES: Well she'd be wrong as usual.

CASILDA: I think the embroidered one is best.

INES: So, the married woman. Well?

COSTANZA: Come on. Tell us. What's it like?

INES: Do you love your husband very much?

CASILDA: We're the happiest couple in Ocaña.
   But let's not speak too soon:
   the wedding cake's not finished yet.

INES: Does he whisper sweet nothings
   into your ear in the dark ?

COSTANZA: Does he keep you awake all night?

CASILDA: I'm wildly in love with him.
   He hurries home to me at night
   hungry, and I'm ready, waiting;
   he has to put the animals to bed
   but we're in each others' arms
   even in the stable. And again
   in the kitchen, on the table,
   with the soup boiling over.
   We feed each other daintily
   like lords and ladies at dinner,
   or we feast from the same dish
   without manners, but with pleasure.
   I drink wine from his mouth.
   He licks my fingers clean.

Everything tastes wonderful.
I'm hungry all the time.
Eventually we fall asleep
curled up like two small children.

INES: A man to hold you through the night –
that's what I want. You're so lucky –

Enter PERIBAÑEZ.

CASILDA: Is everything ready, my love?

PERIBAÑEZ: Your chariot awaits, ladies.

INES: Shall we get on and ride away?

PERIBAÑEZ: What's so funny? What did I say?

CASILDA: Nothing, my love. Are we going now?

PERIBAÑEZ: The cart looks so old and plain and poor.
I wish we had something better;
Blas has good rugs on his seats,
and a new saddlecloth for his mule.

CASILDA: You could borrow them from someone.

INES: Why don't you ask your new-found friend,
the Comendador?

PERIBAÑEZ: Perhaps I should; he owes us a favour
for taking such good care of him.
We're respectable people now;
he might give us something.

CASILDA: What would we lose by asking?

PERIBAÑEZ: It's wrong to go to the city
looking like ordinary villagers.

INES: We'll go and dress.

CASILDA: Perhaps you could also ask –

PERIBAÑEZ: Yes?

CASILDA: – to borrow his feathered hat?

PERIBAÑEZ: No. Not that.

CASILDA: Why not? Is it asking too much?

PERIBAÑEZ: I will not borrow the fancy style
of a nobleman; it would give you airs,
and although it's light as feathers,
would weigh me down with cares.

Exit.

Scene 4

The COMENDADOR's house. Enter the COMENDADOR and LUJAN.

COMENDADOR: They're fine animals. Pedigree?

LUJAN: I've traded some fine mules in my time
but these are the best I've ever seen.

COMENDADOR: The earrings?
How are we going to offer them
and not make him suspicious?

LUJAN: Simply summon him to the house
and tell him how very grateful
you are for all his help –

COMENDADOR: Yes? And?

LUJAN: Sorry, Sir. It makes me laugh
to think a simple man like me
is privy to your private life.

COMENDADOR: I need to use a common man
like you to gain access to her.
If she had been a real lady
I would employ my secretary,
or my steward, or a gentleman

to present her with jewellery,
and purchase diamonds and pearls,
velvet gowns and silk shawls,
and any objects sufficiently
rare and fine to offer her.
Only her low social class
which her beauty easily transcends,
compels me to use your services
to help me win her to my cause.
You still remain my mule-man.
Do not forget your station.

LUJAN: Yes, Sir. You make yourself quite clear.

Enter LEONARDO.

LEONARDO: Excuse me. Peribañez's here.

COMENDADOR: What did you say?

LEONARDO: You remember: the peasant;
he's asking for 'an audience'.
He says he wants to speak to you
'in private if possible'.

LUJAN: Well well well. You're blushing, Sir.

COMENDADOR: The husband of the woman
I am in love with calls on me
and I tremble and quake like a girl.

LUJAN: Can't you face him?

COMENDADOR: Call him through.
Lovers delight in anything
that reminds them of their heart's desire –
even the angry husband
of that purest beauty
who is now my disgrace.

Enter PERIBAÑEZ wearing a cloak.

PERIBAÑEZ: Let me kneel at your feet.

COMENDADOR: Pedro! It is good to see you.
  Let me embrace you.

PERIBAÑEZ: My lord.
  You honour a simple farmer.

COMENDADOR: You are worthy of the best.

PERIBAÑEZ: The very least of your people.

COMENDADOR: Everyone speaks so highly
  of your kindness and good manners;
  and I am greatly in your debt;
  after all, you saved my life.
  So, then: what can we do for you?

PERIBAÑEZ: My lord, as you may remember,
  I am a newly married man.
  Even ordinary men like me
  pay to women the same respects
  as any palace courtier.
  My wife has asked me to take her
  to the August Fiesta in Toledo,
  which draws all kinds of people
  from around Castile.
  It is my wife's first time in the city;
  her cousins are coming with us.
  I want us all to look our best
  and to represent Ocaña well;
  but I lack the proper tapestries
  with the gold and silk embroidery
  displaying the town's emblems
  and your family heraldry.
  So I have come to ask the loan
  of such a cloth to take with us.

COMENDADOR: I see.

PERIBAÑEZ: I beg your forgiveness, Sir,
for my improper boldness
and ignorance of protocol.
Pardon a man in love.

COMENDADOR: Are you happy?

PERIBAÑEZ: Yes, Sir. So much so
I'd not even exchange this shirt
for the scarlet cross of command
you yourself wear on your heart;
I have an honest wife I love;
she's beautiful, and she loves me:
if not as much as I love her
then with a greater love
than the world has ever seen before.

COMENDADOR: You're right to love the woman
who loves you equally
by divine and human law.
That is a pleasure none other can share.
Bring him the Moroccan carpet,
and find eight of the silk hangings
which bear my coat of arms.
And since this is my opportunity
to repay your hospitality
bring him the two new mules I brought
to draw my carriage; and for his wife
if the silversmith has finished,
the earrings I commissioned.

PERIBAÑEZ: I have no words –

COMENDADOR: Then do not speak.

PERIBAÑEZ: Even if I kissed the ground
a thousand times in your good name
I could not possibly repay
the smallest part of this grace.
My wife and I are in your power.

COMENDADOR: Go with him, Leonardo.

They exit.

COMENDADOR: Well? What do you think?

LUJAN: I think luck is on your side.
    He's definitely hooked.

COMENDADOR: Go and saddle my best horse;
    make sure you do it quietly;
    I am going to Toledo in secret
    to follow the woman.

LUJAN: You'll shadow her? That's risky.

COMENDADOR: She steals my heart. I must see her
    no matter what the danger.

Scene 5

Toledo. Enter KING ENRIQUE with CONSTABLE.

CONSTABLE: Toledo is delighted and honoured
    by your most royal visit
    on the eve of our holy Fiesta.

KING: I am enchanted by its beauty
    which I have long wished to admire.

CONSTABLE: And by this splendid welcome
    the city expresses its devotion
    to your most sacred person.

KING: It is the world's eighth marvel:
    the glorious ornament
    in Castile's crown, and the head
    from which the kingdom's body
    draws all its joy and strength.
    Like Rome, the eternal city,
    it reigns from a mountain's height,
    but far surpasses those seven hills

which all centuries celebrate.
I leave this holy cathedral
filled with admiration.

CONSTABLE: If I may be so bold to ask:
might your royal highness lead
tomorrow's holy procession?

KING: As an example of my faith
I shall process with the Queen of Heaven,
and beg her divine favour
in our military campaigns.

Enter a PAGE.

PAGE: Sire, three councillors attend outside.

KING: Let them approach.

Enter three COUNCILLORS.

1ST COUNCILLOR: I kiss your feet and report, Sire,
a swift response to your request
of men and arms for the campaign
from Toledo's many noblemen.

2ND COUNCILLOR: There were no dissenting voices,
My Lord.

3RD COUNCILLOR: All have gladly pledged, Great King,
to the service of your royal arms
a total of one thousand men
and forty thousand crowns.

KING: Tell them I thank Toledo
for her famous generosity.
Are you three gentlemen?

2ND COUNCILLOR: I am indeed.

1ST and 2ND COUNCILLORS: Yes, so are we.

KING: Toledo shall witness my gratitude:
  speak to the Constable tomorrow.
  See that they are rewarded
  with some appropriate office.

Enter INES, COSTANZA, and CASILDA. They are wearing their best clothes but they are clearly from the countryside. They are with PERIBAÑEZ. Their group is cautiously followed by the COMENDADOR, on foot.

CASILDA: Look, there he is; that must be him.

INES: Yes! Enrique the Third!

CASILDA: A fine name.

COSTANZA: And a handsome man.

PERIBAÑEZ: His father was the first King John
  which makes him the grandson
  of Enrique the Second
  who killed King Pedro;
  he was a Guzman on his mother's side,
  and a brave man, or so I heard.
  But during the fatal duel
  he was tripped, and fell to the ground
  and Enrique grasped his dagger
  and plunged it into his heart:
  and that's how he won power.

COSTANZA: Who is that strange-looking man
  the King is talking to?

PERIBAÑEZ: The Constable, I think.

CASILDA: Oh. So that's the King. He's just
  flesh and blood.

COSTANZA: What else did you expect?

CASILDA: I thought his skin would be of silk,
  his hair of gold, with jewels for eyes.

COSTANZA: How could you be that stupid!

COMENDADOR: Like a shadow I follow her sun.
　　This is madness:
　　the King could easily recognise me.
　　He's going in.

Exit the KING and his retinue.

INES: Quick, look: he's going back inside.

COSTANZA: That didn't last long.
　　I couldn't make out from this far
　　if his hair was red or gold.

INES: Costanza, don't you know:
　　Kings are like moving statues;
　　when they appear, we're so impressed
　　we think they're a kind of miracle.
　　But they're just mortal flesh and bone.
　　They eat and shit and go to sleep
　　like the rest of us.

Enter LUJAN with an ARTIST.

LUJAN: There she is.

ARTIST: Which one is she?

LUJAN: Be quiet!
　　I've found you an artist, Sir.

COMENDADOR: Dear friend.

ARTIST: At your service.

COMENDADOR: Have you got your box of paints?

ARTIST: Yes, I've brought all my colours;
　　It's an exciting commission for me.

COMENDADOR: Good. Then bearing in mind
　　the need for absolute discretion;
　　do you see the middle of those three girls?

Sketch me her perfect image
as soon as she has found a seat.

ARTIST: That's not going to be easy.
But I'll do my best.

COMENDADOR: And listen carefully:
if your sketch is good enough
I will commission a portrait:
canvas, oils, frame. The whole works.

ARTIST: Full-length?

COMENDADOR: Her head down to her waist
will be enough. Make sure she looks
exactly as she does right now.

LUJAN: They've found a place to sit.

ARTIST: Then now's my chance.

PERIBAÑEZ: Let's rest here for a while.
We can watch the fireworks.

INES: I heard someone say the Council
are parading the animals through the streets.

CASILDA: We can see everything from here.

COMENDADOR: Draw her in heaven. Add a sky
of the clearest, finest azure;
soft clouds across the horizon,
and a meadow of wild roses.

ARTIST: She's lovely.

LUJAN: She's the Beauty who has turned
my master into the Beast.

ARTIST: The evening light is fading fast.

COMENDADOR: The brightness blazing in her eyes
will illuminate your drawing.

ARTIST: I cannot draw in the dark, Sir.

COMENDADOR: She changes darkness into day
and strikes like lightning at my heart.

End of Act One.

ACT TWO

Scene 1

Ocaña. Four villagers: BLAS, GIL, ANTON, BENITO.

BENITO: Well, you know my view.

BLAS: We certainly do.

GIL: You should write it down.

BLAS: He'd write a book, except he can't.
    He draws a big X when he signs his name
    like a squinting kid at school
    with the pen in the wrong fist.

BENITO: What did he say?

BLAS: And he's deaf –

ANTON: Order, order. Gentlemen!
    It's not right to continue this meeting
    with so few present and correct.
    We are not quorate.

BLAS: Oh yes we are.

ANTON: No we are not. The wording says
    quite clearly there has to be
    all of us and Peribañez here.
    Then we are the quorum.

BENITO: The announcement went up yesterday.

BLAS: Oh, well, that's plenty of notice.

BENITO: Let's start without him. Item One.

ANTON: The fiesta. It was a shambles.

BENITO: Oh, and whose fault was that?

GIL: Gentlemen! The parade went well,

and the Saint was duly honoured.
But we ought to be well aware
that our noble brotherhood
was shown in a very bad light:
there were certain incidents.
Those concerned know who they are.
Those who cannot hold their drink.
Which led to rowdiness and worse.
Profanity. With a firework.
Someone could have been badly hurt.
It's shameful that two grown men
should end up in the fountain
throwing punches, and grappling,
grunting and sputtering and tottering
like two mad dogs in the afternoon
in front of the whole town and his wife!

Silence.

Everything *else* that went so very wrong
can easily be remedied.
And this leads on to my main point:
the good people of Ocaña
show far too little respect
for our patron saint San Roque:
and yet throughout the kingdom
other brotherhoods and parades
get bigger and better and grander.
So why are we afraid to spend
a nominal sum to put this right?

More silence.

Enter PERIBAÑEZ.

PERIBAÑEZ: Gentlemen, I'm sorry I'm late.
Are you waiting for me to start?

ANTON: Ah, you're just the man we need.

BLAS: Welcome back. We've missed you.

GIL: Come and help restore some sense.

PERIBAÑEZ: I doubt if I'll be of much use.

BENITO: Sit down here, next to me.

GIL: Where have you been, then?

PERIBAÑEZ: In Toledo. My wife and I
    went for the Fiesta.

ANTON: Impressive?

PERIBAÑEZ: I can honestly say
    I saw heaven on earth:
    the Cathedral, and the Virgin –
    only a visiting angel
    with a silver chisel
    could have made her so lovely.
    The procession through the streets
    was truly magnificent;
    we saw all kinds of dignitaries
    behaving in the courtly style,
    glittering in their jewellery
    and glowing in so much red and gold.
    And the great event was crowned
    by the presence of the King.
    It was hard to see through the crowds,
    and we were standing far away,
    but he was smaller than I imagined.
    The Masters of the Grand Orders
    of Alcantara and Calatrava
    are planning a new campaign
    and raising a great army
    against the Moors, to wipe them out –
    although they always fight back hard;
    they're tough and fearless soldiers.

    How did things go here?
    Was the fiesta a success?

GIL: Without you, our simple brotherhood
    got almost everything wrong.

PERIBAÑEZ: I wanted to get back in time
    for the last day. But Casilda
    was determined to pray
    to the Virgin herself, every day
    for the whole of holy week.
    She would not leave the shrine.
    What were you all discussing
    before I interrupted you?

ANTON: The dignity of the brotherhood
    and those that fail its standards.
    But you have given me an idea;
    we need to elect a new steward
    and you would be just the man,
    with your influence in high places.
    I'm talking about your new-found friend:
    the generous Comendador.

BENITO: That's exactly what *I* thought
    as soon as I saw you come in.

BLAS: Anyone against?

GIL: I think he's the one. Next year
    he can take on the responsibility
    and put everything to rights.

PERIBAÑEZ: You know I am just married
    and should refuse your offer;
    but since you've honoured me
    so generously, how can I say no?
    Here and now I vow to serve
    with all the power at my command
    our patron saint San Roque.

GIL: Good. Now I have a proposal.

PERIBAÑEZ: Tell me what I need to do.

GIL: I would like to propose
   the ordering of a new saint.
   It should be bigger and better
   than our present model
   by at least twice the height
   and therefore easier to see
   above the heads of the crowd.

PERIBAÑEZ: A good proposal. Anton?

ANTON: I agree. The saint we have now
   is far too small and old for us.
   We need one which will really inspire
   true feelings of devotion
   in everyone who looks at it,
   rather than jokes and laughter.
   The old one is falling to pieces:
   his dog looks mangy and bald;
   the loaf of bread has been broken off;
   and the guardian angel
   has rotted all down one side.

BLAS: And his two-fingered blessing?
   One of the fingers is missing.

PERIBAÑEZ: So then, Blas, do you agree?

BLAS: No. I think you and Anton should go
   straight back to Toledo today
   taking the old fellow with you,
   and commission a decent painter
   to fix him up as good as new.
   To me it makes no sort of sense
   to spend good money on a new saint
   when this one can be repaired.
   Besides, he's been our saint for years.
   He's a bit buggered like the rest of us.
   But a bigger saint isn't holier,
   and wouldn't make our souls better.

PERIBAÑEZ: I'm afraid Blas is right, because
    our brotherhood is short of funds.
    How can we get him there and back?
    I'm in and out of the city
    like a man of important affairs.

ANTON: We could wrap him in a blanket
    so he won't get knocked about
    and tie him on my mule. Or yours.

PERIBAÑEZ: So. If I'm to leave today
    we should adjourn the meeting now.

BLAS: Before we go, dear brotherhood,
    I want to make it quite clear –
    in case there's any doubt at all –
    that I'll pay my share of a new saint
    if that's what everyone prefers.

BENITO: Well, hark at the voice of charity!

PERIBAÑEZ: Anton, let's go.
    I need to say goodbye to Casilda.

ANTON: I'll get the old chap ready for his journey.

PERIBAÑEZ: She's not going to be pleased:
    I know I have a good excuse,
    but she'll say it's wrong to go away
    just as the harvest is ready,
    and the workers have to be hired,
    and all the man's work's left to her.

Scene 2

The COMENDADOR's house.

COMENDADOR: So tell me everything.

LEONARDO: The news is: I have conquered.
    Ines came home with Casilda

like the rising sun but gentler,
and much less glaring and angry;
I walked up and down past her door
hoping to catch a glimpse of her,
and show her I was interested.
I passed as often as I dared –
as you know these common people
are the worst gossips in the world.
Later, I found an opportunity
to introduce myself to her
at a dance in the street;
I performed my love speech
which I had prepared earlier
and she blushed so deeply in reply
as if I'd touched her with my finger.
Then I found another chance
to carry home my advantage
when I met her, a few days later,
walking out to the fields;
once more I impressed the maid
with all my swindling sorrows.
This time she listened carefully
to every counterfeit sigh and vow
I whispered into her red ear.
And suddenly she promised
to be my honest little lover.
About our main plan of action
regarding her own dear cousin,
she wouldn't agree to help us out
or do anything against the girl,
until I gave her to understand
I would marry her, but *only* if
my master agreed to the wedding:
and if you did not give your consent
then there was nothing I could do
and the wedding would be off.
And that is how I left her;

if we need to get to Casilda
then the cousin's the best way in.

COMENDADOR: This is absurd. I'm handsome, rich,
and I really am in love with her.
What more could a woman want?
I wish there were a simpler way
to conquer her scorn and contempt.
But she has a heart of stone.

LEONARDO: So she's still resisting you?

COMENDADOR: I followed her to Toledo
like a shadow trailing the sun.
When I caught her on her own
I revealed myself to her
and confessed my pain and sorrow;
but her lovely face turned pale as if
she was staring Death in the face.
Then she blushed red as a rose,
then quickly froze like snow again,
and a fury grew inside her.
I tried to plead in silence,
my eyes weeping true tears
to show how she had wounded me
by her anger; but to no avail.
She seemed more beautiful than ever.
In a moment of insanity
I commissioned a drawing of her.

LEONARDO: Was it a good likeness?

COMENDADOR: So good that I commissioned
a full-length portrait, which will hang
where I can see it all the time;
while I cannot possess the original
in all her living beauty
her cold image will console me.
It should be finished today;
I want you to collect it.

LEONARDO: I am sorry you torment yourself
　　over a woman who will submit
　　as soon as she understands what you want.
　　'Women will not speak the word
　　but they will always do the deed.'
　　Let me talk to Ines;
　　I'll see what can be done.

COMENDADOR: Anything she can do to help
　　would mean more than the world to me.

Enter LUJAN dressed as a harvester.

LUJAN: Pst. Excuse me, Sir.

COMENDADOR: Lujan?

LUJAN: Are you alone?

COMENDADOR: Only Leonardo's here.

LUJAN: Great news, Sir.

COMENDADOR: Where have you been?
　　Why are you wearing that outfit?

LUJAN: This? I'm in disguise, Sir.
　　Humble Labourer. Man of the Earth.
　　I went to Peribañez
　　who didn't even recognize me,
　　and has hired me for the harvest.
　　So I'm sleeping in his house,
　　incognito; he has no idea.

COMENDADOR: I wish I were sleeping there too.

LUJAN: I'm not sure you'd like it, Sir:
　　we start at dawn tomorrow
　　and work through until dark.
　　But I think I've found a remedy
　　for your heart's love-agony.
　　Peribañez has gone away:
　　he won't be home until tomorrow night

at the very earliest.
So tonight, when everyone's asleep,
I'll be waiting for your signal
to open the front door from inside,
and guide you to the bedroom
where this invincible woman sleeps
in her warm bed, dreaming of you.

COMENDADOR: You will be rewarded for this.

LUJAN: All I ask is your happiness, Sir.

COMENDADOR: Excellent, man.
See how the way to happiness
suddenly runs smoothly
like the calm after the storm:
the jealous fool is far away,
and with you there inside his house
nothing could be simpler.
The door stands open wide.
Have you searched the house
from top to bottom?

LUJAN: I've even seen where she sleeps.

COMENDADOR: You've been inside her private room?
What did you see? What was she doing?

LUJAN: She was embroidering in the sun;
the clear light played upon her face
as she sat among her flowers,
singing a simple melody.
Your hangings were there on the walls;
seeing them like that, I thought:
'trophies of love surrendered in war
to the goddess of ardour.'

COMENDADOR: No; they hang there as the sign
of the triumphant conquest
which is now within my grasp.
No-one must see you here with me.

Go back and wait. I will prepare
for the night and its sweet victory.

LUJAN: Should Leonardo come as well?

COMENDADOR: Yes: he might be useful
in case anything goes wrong.

Scene 3

PERIBAÑEZ's house. CASILDA and INES.

CASILDA: Ines, I'm scared.
There's no moon.
It's so dark. And quiet.
I don't like Pedro being away.
Would you sleep here with me tonight?

INES: I'll have to ask my parents –

CASILDA: You're not a child. They know where you are.

INES: Don't be like that. I'll run over
and ask them now.

CASILDA: It's much too late to go ourselves.
I'll send a messenger
to let them know you're safe.
I promise.

INES: As you like, cousin.

CASILDA: In your whole life you have never
done me a greater favour.

INES: You're not used to sleeping alone.
But you'll still be afraid with me here;
and if anything bad happens tonight
I won't be any use to you:
I can't pretend to be your man
with all his handy bravery
to hold you safe in his muscular arms.
And as for a real intruder:

a sheathed sword sets me quivering,
and if it's drawn, naked, and dangerous –
I go to pieces and pass out.

CASILDA: There's nothing to be frightened of
is there? We're safe inside the house
and the men will sleep by the door.

INES: Being alone is the worst:
when fear won't let you sleep.
But as you said:
there's nothing to be afraid of.

CASILDA: But I am afraid.
I'll lie awake in the small hours;
in the dark love turns to fear,
and jealousy steals into my heart.

INES: What could he possibly do
to worry you in Toledo?

CASILDA: Don't you see? Jealousy
is like the air; it's everywhere.
It lives and breathes in everything
and no-one can escape its power.

INES: Jealous love will make you crazy
according to the song I heard.

CASILDA: What did you say on my wedding day?
Jealousy is the price we pay
for love? Now I see that's true.
He could be up to anything
in Toledo. Anything at all.

INES: Now that you mention it,
the women there *are* beautiful...

CASILDA: The workmen are here. Come inside.

*Enter LLORENTE and MENDO, two of the harvesters worn
out with the day's labour.*

LLORENTE: I'm too old for this.

MENDO: Someone put me to bed.

LLORENTE: Up with the sun. Down with the sun.

MENDO: Help me. I can't feel anything.

LLORENTE: You'll feel it tomorrow. Stiff?
    You'll be stiff as a dead donkey.

MENDO: Don't talk about tomorrow.

LLORENTE: Chose your spot and go to sleep.

CASILDA: The men are going to sleep now.

INES: Perhaps you should send Sancho
    to stand watch at the garden door?

LLORENTE: The mistress is closing up the house.
    Now her husband's away for the night
    and she's left in charge, you'll see
    she'll be hurrying us out to work
    before the crack of dawn.

Enter BARTOLO and CHAPARRO, harvesters.

BARTOLO: Evening, lads.

LLORENTE: Bartolo. Chaparro. Alright?

BARTOLO: No I'm not. It's just not on.
    Tomorrow I have to mow
    the edge of the whole meadow.

CHAPARRO: You'd better be up early, then.
    Mendo, Llorente: sweet dreams.

LLORENTE: Sweet dreams? I'll have nightmares
    about scything away all day
    in a field that goes on forever
    under a midday sun that never moves.

MENDO: (*Asleep.*) Grab and cut, grab and cut...

CHAPARRO: Ah, good work has a shine to it.
　　Is he going to talk all night?
　　Someone sing or tell us a story
　　before we nod off.

MENDO: Grab and grab and grab and grab...

They suddenly shout at MENDO.

OY!

MENDO: COMING!

BARTOLO: That woke you up.

MENDO: What's happening? What time is it?

LLORENTE: You just dropped off.

MENDO: Sometimes I wish morning came
　　just once in a whole year.

Enter HELIPE and LUJAN, harvesters.

HELIPE: Move over there: let's have some space.

MENDO: Hey, Helipe. How's it going?

HELIPE: Horrible.

LUJAN: Is there a space for me?

CHAPARRO: Over there; you can sleep by the door
　　and keep the draft out.

BARTOLO: We're about to have a song.

CHAPARRO: And a bedtime story too.

LUJAN: Oh good. Sing the song first,
　　then I'll tell a little tale
　　of wicked lust and true romance.

LLORENTE: I'll start off the singing, shall I?

The green grass grows
slim and fine
for the young girl
who will be mine

The green grass grows
sweet and new
for the bride who loves
her husband true

The green grass grows
bright and strong
for the woman
who sings love's song

The green grass grows
without fear
love comes again
every year

The green grass blows
in slow green waves
over the hills
and love's stone graves

LUJAN: That worked like a dream; look at them:
    snoring already.
    What about my story?

LLORENTE: Save it for tomorrow. I'm joining them,
    even if this floor's no bed of roses.
    Goodnight, God Bless.

LUJAN: Sweet dreams! Goodnight! Dead to the world.
    I could easily fall asleep –
    this manual work is killing me –
    but I've got to stay alert.
    Night, I entrust our hopes to you.

A whistle is heard. LUJAN quietly opens the door.

Enter the COMENDADOR and LEONARDO.

173

COMENDADOR: What about this lot?

LUJAN: Sleeping like babies.
Nothing's going to wake them up.

COMENDADOR: Do you know the way?

LUJAN: Even in the dark.

COMENDADOR: Show me.

LUJAN: Leonardo must keep watch.

LEONARDO: Fine. I'll wait here.

LUJAN: Follow me.

COMENDADOR: Shine on me, stars of luck and love.

They exit.

LLORENTE: (*Starts awake.*) Mendo. Mendo! Wake up.
Someone's broken into the house;
they're creeping about in the dark.

MENDO: I thought this might happen.
Is this how they show respect
to a good man like Peribañez?

LLORENTE: They're not locals;
one was wearing a gold-lined cloak.

MENDO: Gold-lined? The Comendador?

LLORENTE: Let's shout for help.

MENDO: No! No. Let's just keep very quiet.
It's none of our business.

LLORENTE: Perhaps you're right.
How do you know it's him?

MENDO: No-one else in Ocaña
would dare to walk in here at night.

LLORENTE: I could have told him: there's always strife
with a young and pretty wife.

MENDO: They're coming back. Pretend you're asleep.

Enter the COMENDADOR and LUJAN.

COMENDADOR: Leonardo?

LEONARDO: Yes?

COMENDADOR: Where are you?

LEONARDO: Boo. Success?

COMENDADOR: No.

LEONARDO: What happened?

COMENDADOR: She's double-locked the bedroom door.

LEONARDO: So why don't you just knock?

COMENDADOR: Don't be stupid;
    it would wake the whole house up.

LEONARDO: Nothing will wake this lot up Sir:
    too much wine and too much work.
    A dancing donkey wouldn't stir them now.
    Ssh. Listen. Someone's opening
    the door onto the balcony.

COMENDADOR: Now everything is going wrong.

LEONARDO: Perhaps it's her.

COMENDADOR: Of course it's her, you fool.

CASILDA is at the window in a shawl.

CASILDA: Friends, can it be dawn so soon?

COMENDADOR: My lady, the sky will soon be bright
    and we must go to work in the fields.
    We are sorry to see you alone.
    Your husband cannot love you
    or he would not have left you
    defenceless and alone all night.
    If the Comendador of Ocaña

– who I know loves you with all his heart,
despite your cold behaviour;
if the Comendador himself
– who I believe you may admire –
were as lucky as your husband,
he'd never leave you in an empty house;
not even if the King himself
summoned him to appear at court.
The man who dares abandon you
has broken love's first law.

CASILDA: Stranger from another place;
you have come at harvest time,
guided by the summer's heat.
Who put these thoughts into your head?
Take your work clothes, and your coat,
tie your thick gloves to your belt,
pick up your sickle, and leave the house;
go through the dew and the dawn birds
out to the fields and start your work.
Cut the sheaves and tie them tight,
take care not to damage them,
and work until the sun has gone.
But when the evening star appears
do not attempt to return to this place
for nothing good will come of this.
The Comendador of Ocaña
should woo a fine young lady
who does not dress in village clothes
but wears her hair coiffured in curls
and a starched ruff, and a silver net,
not an ordinary straw hat.
She is not jolted in a wooden cart
but glides about in a silver coach.
She whispers sweet nothings to him
in her witty love letters,
not common words of anger.
Her perfume is expensive:
not brambles and wild flowers.

Even if the Comendador
loved me with all his life and wealth,
and even if love and honour
were nothing but a tissue of lies
told by a desperate lover –
I would still love Peribañez
for his plain clothes and words
more than the Comendador
in all his silks and jewellery.
I love to see him riding home
across the fields he's harvested
with the dogs running at his heels,
and the gold sun setting at his back.
And I revere San Roque's stone cross
more than I ever will adore
the cross of Santiago
stitched in red across the heart
of the brave Comendador.
So go now, stranger, on your way.
If Peribañez finds you here
you will be dead.

COMENDADOR: Casilda. Hush. Listen to me.
I am the Comendador.
Please open the door. Look here:
two strings of pearls. For you.
And this – a jewelled necklace.
If I could lay it on your neck –

CASILDA: Wake up, wake up everyone.
Dawn is calling. Time to work.
Wake up!

BARTOLO: No, it can't be –

CHAPARRO: Oh sweet Jesus –

CASILDA: Tonight, when you come back to eat
I'll give the hardest worker
an extra bottle of good wine.

She withdraws.

LUJAN: Run Sir, before they see you here.

COMENDADOR: The heartless and ungrateful bitch.
Though it may cost me everything,
honour, wealth, even my life,
she will submit to my desire
and weep for her lost honour
when it is worth no more than dust.

The COMENDADOR, LUJAN and LEONARDO exit.

BARTOLO: Wake up lads. It's getting late.

CHAPARRO: Helipe. Come on, wake up.

HELIPE: Why are the stars still shining?

LLORENTE: Right, let's get going. On your feet.
We don't want the mistress to say
we're idle when the master's away.

Scene 4

Toledo. Enter PERIBAÑEZ, the ARTIST and ANTON.

PERIBAÑEZ: Kind Sir, yesterday I saw
among the icons and portraits
one of a girl which caught my eye:
perhaps because she had such grace,
perhaps because, like me, the girl
came from the country. It haunts me:
now you have our saint in hand
would you show it to me again?

ARTIST: You've a good eye. She's a country girl.
A beautiful simplicity.

PERIBAÑEZ: Could you bring it out to me?
I'd like Anton to see it too.

ANTON: I noticed it before.
But I'd be glad to see it again.

PERIBAÑEZ: Would you fetch it?

ARTIST: Certainly.

He goes.

PERIBAÑEZ: You'll see the face of an angel.

ANTON: I know why you want to look at it.

PERIBAÑEZ: Oh?

ANTON: I think it has occurred to you
    she looks just like Casilda.

PERIBAÑEZ: Is Casilda really as beautiful?

ANTON: You're her husband. You praise her.

Enter the ARTIST with a large portrait of CASILDA.

ARTIST: Here she is.

PERIBAÑEZ: (*Aside.*) And my dishonour.

ARTIST: Isn't she perfect?

PERIBAÑEZ: Perfect. What do you think, Anton?

ANTON: She's beautiful in your eyes
    and also admirable to the world.

PERIBAÑEZ: Anton, would you go ahead
    and saddle up the horses?
    I'll be along in a moment.

ANTON: (*Aside.*) I'm no expert, but that girl
    is definitely Casilda;
    and he's on fire with jealousy.

He leaves.

PERIBAÑEZ: What a work of art this is:
    the sparkling eyes, the lovely mouth.
    Where does the woman come from?

ARTIST: Don't you recognise her face?

PERIBAÑEZ: There's something there – but I'm not sure.

ARTIST: No? Perhaps the likeness
isn't as good as I thought:
in fact she's from your village.

PERIBAÑEZ: From Ocaña?

ARTIST: Yes.

PERIBAÑEZ: I see. Now that you mention it –

ARTIST: Yes?

PERIBAÑEZ: She does remind me of someone;
a woman who's recently married.

ARTIST: I don't know who she really is;
my client was most insistent
that she should not be aware of me.
I had to follow her around
in the crowds during holy week
until I could do a quick sketch:
it was all very secretive.
Later I worked the charcoal sketch
into this finished portrait.

PERIBAÑEZ: So who commissioned this?

ARTIST: I really can't say.

PERIBAÑEZ: Let me guess –

ARTIST: My client is an important man.
He wishes to remain –

PERIBAÑEZ: Oh, obviously –

ARTIST: – and I must respect his wishes.

PERIBAÑEZ: The Comendador of Ocaña?

ARTIST: Sir, I don't know what to say.

PERIBAÑEZ: Why, you have said nothing, Sir.

ARTIST: Knowing that she is unaware
    of the love that great man bears her,
    I believe I can reveal the truth.

PERIBAÑEZ: So the woman herself has no idea?

ARTIST: None at all. In fact, I believe
    she must be faithfully involved
    with some other gentleman;
    perhaps she was aware of me
    because she was so elusive;
    one moment she would sit down,
    then next she vanished into thin air.

PERIBAÑEZ: I am returning to Ocaña today:
    would you allow me to deliver
    the picture to its owner?

ARTIST: I have not been paid yet.

PERIBAÑEZ: I will pay the full amount.

ARTIST: The Comendador would be displeased.
    He is sending his man tomorrow
    to fetch it in person, and pay my fee.

    Can I offer any other help?

PERIBAÑEZ: While you are repairing the saint
    I'll continue to admire your work.

ARTIST: As you wish.

He exits.

PERIBAÑEZ: Who am I now? Another man.
    I cannot bear to look at her.
    How will I ever look at her?
    But if she has no part in this
    why should I reveal the pain
    tearing my heart to pieces?
    A husband's tormented jealousy
    is a monster of ugliness

and must never be displayed,
but disguise itself in silence.
It is wrong that another man
desires to possess my wife;
it is much worse that the very man
who should protect my honour
dishonours me. By all that's right
he should shield me from this harm.
He is a rich man, I am poor;
but if he plans to steal my wife,
my honour and my happiness,
then I am left without a choice:
I will have to kill him. Yes,
Casilda's still faithful to me;
but once a rumour is set loose
everyone will know my shame.
I was so simple: I believed
her beauty would bring me happiness.
I was wrong to marry her.

Scene 5

The COMENDADOR's house. Enter LEONARDO and the CO-MENDADOR.

LEONARDO: You sent for me, Sir?

COMENDADOR: The King has written to me,
   commanding troops to be conscripted
   from Ocaña.

LEONARDO: So what will you do?

COMENDADOR: What we always do at times like this:
   make a public proclamation
   and sign up all the local men.
   We need two hundred divided
   into two separate companies:
   a hundred men, a hundred gentlemen.

LEONARDO: Why not all gentlemen?

COMENDADOR: Because peasants cost us nothing.
But you've also missed the point:
I shall appoint Peribañez
captain of the hundred men.
And he'll go marching off to war
And with one clever plot device
I write him out of the story.

LEONARDO: Lovers make the strangest plans.

COMENDADOR: Love is warfare: every move
is strategy. Is he back yet?

LEONARDO: He was expected home tonight.
Lujan says Casilda's terrified;
Ines told me she's decided
to pretend nothing happened.
She doesn't want his feelings hurt.
Seeing how upset she was
Ines kept her own council;
but she'll soon find another chance
to tell her what she really thinks.

COMENDADOR: Casilda has a heart of ice.
From the first day I saw her
I have been a crippled man
begging for the cure for love.

LEONARDO: Troy once seemed impregnable
and yet it fell to a wooden horse.
It's simple: village girls are shy.
They always say 'no thank you, Sir'
to the very thing they most desire.
You have to keep working at them.
So send him honourably to war
and see how fast your wish comes true.

COMENDADOR: Perhaps fortune will smile on me.
How often have I proved myself
fearless on the battlefield?
Now the strangest fears assail me.

LEONARDO: You should ignore your fear's advice;
    who ever loved without hope?

He exits.

COMENDADOR: I have no hope; I twist and twine
    like ivy round her life, but she
    remains impervious to me,
    a living statue of flesh and bone.
    And since my life depends on her
    thus I am doomed to die alone.
    Goddess of Love, hear my prayer:
    when I am dust, turn her to stone.

Exit.

Scene 6

Near Ocaña. PERIBAÑEZ and ANTON.

PERIBAÑEZ: Anton, go on home alone.

ANTON: What about you?

PERIBAÑEZ: I have some work to finish here.

ANTON: But Casilda will be worried –

PERIBAÑEZ: I need to see my harvesters;
    they're working in the fields just there.

ANTON: Wouldn't it be better to go
    straight home to her?

PERIBAÑEZ: Hurry home, and since you're passing,
    tell her I've stayed behind to see
    the progress of the harvest.

ANTON: (*Aside.*) This is not right.
    But I don't want him to see
    I know exactly what he's thinking.
    God speed.

Exit ANTON.

PERIBAÑEZ: Farewell.

Why do I stop and fear my home
like a cold hearth full of ashes?
Casilda, you are innocent.
So why do I avoid you? Love,
your grace must shape my destiny.
If you were not so beautiful
our noble lord Comendador
would not be crazed with love.
In a dream my life was simple once:
this was my land, my threshing stones;
my own hands dug and planted here,
this harvest, stooked and dry, was mine.
My heart was light with happiness.

I hear their voices. I must hide.

Shouts off, as if they are reaping.

MENDO: Hey, Bartolo, it's time to eat.

BARTOLO: He who works not shall not eat.

MENDO: I'm working like a dog –

LLORENTE: A thirsty dog?

MENDO: I could drink a river.

CHAPARRO: And you'd still be yapping for more.

PERIBAÑEZ: Everything here is familiar;
and everything fills me with sorrow.

MENDO: Hey, Llorente, sing us a song:
the one about the master's wife.

PERIBAÑEZ: Now everything I fear comes true.

LLORENTE: (*Sings.*)
Peribañez's wife

is beautiful and true;
but our Lord of Ocaña
tells her 'I love you.'
Day and night he woos her
while her husband is away.
But listen to her wise reply:
I love my Peribañez more
in his coat so grey and old
than you my Lord Comendador
in your cloak of shining gold.

MENDO: Did you compose that yourself?

LLORENTE: It was better than listening to you.

MENDO: You're a troubadour, my friend...

They exit.

PERIBAÑEZ: Suddenly I can breathe again.
The song has told the truth;
Casilda has proved faithful.
But my honour still remains in doubt
if a labourer puts it in a song.

Scene 7

PERIBAÑEZ's house. CASILDA and INES.

CASILDA: You must be mad –

INES: Let him in.

CASILDA: What a terrible thing to say.

INES: Casilda, all you have to do –

CASILDA: Don't. I won't listen to this.

INES: If you would only listen to me
you'd realise your mistake:

this has nothing to do with you.
What I have to say concerns *me*.

CASILDA: You?

INES: Yes, me.

CASILDA: I'm sorry. I'm losing my mind.

INES: Leonardo is in love with me
and wants us to be married.

CASILDA: No, Ines.

INES: Yes, Casilda.

CASILDA: Can't you see? He's deceiving you!

INES: I'm as dear as life to him.

CASILDA: You're about as dear as his master's gold.

INES: Why do you doubt his love for me?

CASILDA: These men seduce us with their love,
take what they want, and then they leave.

INES: I have his signed guarantee.

CASILDA: Ines, this town is full of women
who are eligible and pretty
with rich dowries; but you
are sadly not a rich, fine lady.

INES: If you speak to him like that,
so haughty and contemptuous,
you'll ruin my only chance.
I need the Comendador's consent.

CASILDA: Can't you see he's using you?
He's convinced you he's panting
with love, but all he truly wants
is to help his Master get to me.

INES: Why is it impossible
    he truly loves me for myself?
    And who are you to be so proud?
    Why can't you spare him a few kind words?

CASILDA: If virtue matters, if truth exists,
    if life itself is dear to you,
    you will not repeat his name,
    and you must never let him in
    past the door of this house again.
    I will not hear what he has to say;
    his talk leads only to a bad end.

Enter PERIBAÑEZ carrying some bags.

PERIBAÑEZ: Casilda.

CASILDA: My love.

PERIBAÑEZ: Are you well?

CASILDA: I missed you so much.
    How was the journey?

PERIBAÑEZ: It was difficult. But now I'm home
    I feel well again. Hello, Ines.

INES: Welcome home.

PERIBAÑEZ: What more do I need
    if I have you both together?

CASILDA: Ines has kept me company
    while you have been away.

PERIBAÑEZ: I'm grateful for your care.

CASILDA: So have you brought me anything?

PERIBAÑEZ: Nothing but love. Some devotion.
    Perhaps a little adoration.

CASILDA: How kind. And maybe something else?

PERIBAÑEZ: The old saint weighed me down so much
    I could not carry all the gifts
    I wanted to buy for you.

CASILDA: Oh.

PERIBAÑEZ: But I did manage to find a place
    for these new shoes, with pearl buckles –
    and these soft velvet berets –
    and two long belts for your dresses
    with silver decorations.

CASILDA: Thank you, thank you.

PERIBAÑEZ: I nearly had an accident.
    I'm lucky to be alive here now.

CASILDA: Don't frighten me. What happened?

PERIBAÑEZ: I lost my footing on a steep path
    and fell way down, onto the rocks.

CASILDA: What?

PERIBAÑEZ: If I hadn't called out to our saint
    whose awkward weight caused me to fall
    in the first place, I might be dead.

CASILDA: Stop: you make my blood run cold.

PERIBAÑEZ: I promised him all the things I love
    in this house, for his shrine;
    so tomorrow I'm taking down
    these tapestries. I'll hang them up
    on his chapel walls, in thanksgiving.

CASILDA: If they were made of gold and pearls
    I would not try to stop you.

PERIBAÑEZ: It is best. They should not be here.
    They display the arms of another man.
    The town gossips must not whisper
    about the ordinary farmer

who decorates his innocent house
with the Comendador's trophies.
His crest and feathers are out of place
among our ploughs and implements.
The cross pinned above our table
must be of twisted straw, not gold.
What barbarians have I killed,
that I can claim such heraldry?
All I want shown on my own walls
are pictures of the holy saints,
the Annunciation, the Assumption,
Saint Peter in his bare hermitage,
Saint Sebastian in his agony.
Casilda, let's go in to dinner.
And prepare our bed as well.

CASILDA: Are you feeling ill?

PERIBAÑEZ: Now I'm fine.

Enter LUJAN.

LUJAN: I have a message here for you.
It comes from the Comendador.

PERIBAÑEZ: For me? What does he want? It's late.

LUJAN: You'll find out when you speak to him.

PERIBAÑEZ: You look familiar. Are you the man
who came to this house two days ago
looking for work ?

LUJAN: Perhaps you have mistaken me;
I was here with the Comendador.

PERIBAÑEZ: Don't be surprised at my poor memory:
there are so many men around here.

LUJAN: (*Aside.*) This isn't looking good.

PERIBAÑEZ: (*Aside.*) Why has he sent me a message tonight?
Honour is man's hardest task
and his most fragile triumph;
it is as clear and true as glass,
but shatters at the lightest touch.

End of Act Two.

ACT THREE

Scene 1

The COMENDADOR and LEONARDO.

COMENDADOR: Quickly, tell me everything
   that happened in Toledo.

LEONARDO: I'll be as brief as possible –

COMENDADOR: Then start at once –

LEONARDO: My story takes some time to tell.

COMENDADOR: Listen: I'm a dying man.
   Make this fast as possible.

LEONARDO: Certainly. King Enrique the Third,
   named the Just (and juster he
   than even Cato and Aristides),
   in fourteen hundred and six,
   holds court in Madrid. Then suddenly
   dispatches come, informing him
   the Moor of Granada's broken truce –
   tributes unpaid, castles held back –
   so he resolves to attack, and fight
   a glorious campaign of wars.
   He calls upon his relatives
   the Kings of Aragon and Navarre.
   He summons his high council too
   of bishops and earls, of lords and knights,
   good men from all across the land
   together with their lawyers who
   justly and appropriately agree
   the disposition of arms and men.
   Among them were –

COMENDADOR: When I said tell me everything
   I didn't expect a heroic epic.

Isn't the point simply this:
the King is marching south today
with the best men in the kingdom
intending to attack the Moors?

LEONARDO: Precisely.

COMENDADOR: Good. Now listen carefully;
    I spoke to Peribañez,
    to inform him I had elected him
    captain of a hundred men,
    and so he should prepare at once.
    Of course this seemed a great honour,
    so he accepted gratefully
    (little realising my true intent).
    He's spent his savings on new clothes
    and yesterday his company
    – if such a rout deserve the word –
    paraded publicly in the square.
    Lujan reliably informs me
    they're marching off to war today.

LEONARDO: He's leaving his wife to her fate, then.
    Is she still as cruel as ever?
    Still chaste below the waist,
    her woman's softness turned to stone?

COMENDADOR: Yes. But when her husband's gone
    I shall surely influence her
    like quiet-flowing water
    that shapes the hardest stone
    in time to its desire.

    Drums.

LEONARDO: Whose are the drums?

COMENDADOR: I'm sure they're his:
    The captain leads his loyal troops.
    Fetch your weapons and your men
    and parade them in the square;

then we will have some fun
with this home-made gentleman.

*Enter a company of VILLAGE MEN, armed in a comically
improvised way, followed by PERIBAÑEZ with sword and
dagger.*

PERIBAÑEZ: My Lord, I could not depart
until I had seen you.

COMENDADOR: I appreciate the courtesy.

PERIBAÑEZ: I go to serve you, Sir.

COMENDADOR: You serve my Lord the King.

PERIBAÑEZ: The King and you.

COMENDADOR: Indeed.

PERIBAÑEZ: My lord, I serve the King by rights,
and you because you honour me.
How else but by your honour
could I have risen as I have,
from an ordinary farmer
to a Captain under the King?
How else but by your honour
could I be marching for the King
under his royal banner,
who is too great to know my name
and whose exalted majesty
is beyond the understanding
and reach of my poor senses?
May God protect and save you.

COMENDADOR: And may he guard you on your way.

PERIBAÑEZ: Am I dressed correctly, Sir?

COMENDADOR: Perfectly. We are now the same.

PERIBAÑEZ: I have one wish. Will you grant it?

COMENDADOR: Speak, and we'll see.

PERIBAÑEZ: I'd ask you to buckle on my sword
so I leave with public honour.
I ask you to use your own hands, Sir;
this is the custom that bestows
on me the name of Gentleman.

COMENDADOR: You are a man of spirit, and, I expect,
a brave soldier. Give me your sword.

PERIBAÑEZ: Here, Sir.

COMENDADOR: Bear this weapon for my sake.

BARTOLO: Get down on your knees, he's knighting him.

BLAS: What will happen if I don't?

BARTOLO: Plenty if you don't look humble.

BLAS: Will he do the business with the sword?
You're old and wise – you ought to know.

BARTOLO: I know about saddling my old mule;
not about arming gentlemen-knights.

COMENDADOR: And now I've buckled on your sword.

PERIBAÑEZ: And then?

COMENDADOR: Swear to God and to the King
to serve them truly with this sword.

PERIBAÑEZ: This I swear: to wear this sword
throughout my life, and from this day
always to keep it at my side
to fight and guard my honour.
And as I leave my home for war –
at your gracious request, my Lord –
I entrust into your noble care

my precious wife and all my land.
You know they matter more to me
than my own life which I risk for you.
I bid you to watch over her
and vow to keep her safe from harm.
I know you know what honour is;
we choose it over life itself
knowing its true value.
Today you arm me as a knight,
and now I know what honour is;
before, I lived in ignorance.
But now that we are equals,
guard her with your life. You must
accept from me this simple charge;
if not I'll fight for my revenge.

COMENDADOR: If I should fail to guard your wife
loyally, I grant you the right
to lodge a full complaint. Farewell.

PERIBAÑEZ: March on, men. Come what come may.

Exit, marching after his men.

COMENDADOR: I am astonished by his speech;
he seems to be establishing
grounds for a case against me.
No; I was imagining it.
How guilty thoughts tarnish the mind!
Tonight this woman will be mine;
I'll force her to desire me;
then she who is destroying me
will die before tomorrow's dawn.

Scene 2

PERIBAÑEZ's house. Enter CASILDA, COSTANZA and INES.

COSTANZA: So it's true he's leaving you?

CASILDA: Yes, he's going to the war
   and leaving me here confused, alone.

INES: Now, don't cry: not everyone
   is married to a real Captain.

CASILDA: He doesn't deserve such titles.

COSTANZA: That's true; usually real gentleman
   are put in charge of working men.
   I hear they've been ordered to march
   only to Toledo, and then to wait.

CASILDA: If they were going any further
   do you think I'd still be alive?

INES: Here come the drums; it must be him.

   *Drum beats. Enter PERIBAÑEZ with banner and SOL-
   DIERS.*

BARTOLO: See those girls on the balcony?
   That's a sight to raise the old beast,
   even though I'm past it now.

PERIBAÑEZ: You're not that old Bartolo.

BARTOLO: I don't get the urges any more.
   Sorry to say the flesh is weak...

PERIBAÑEZ: Surely there's life still stirring
   under that old coat of yours?

BARTOLO: Good Lord, Captain! Once upon a time
   it was all I ever thought about.

CASILDA: Captain of my sadness.

PERIBAÑEZ: Lady of the balcony;
   I hold this banner for your sake.

CASILDA: Are you leaving Ocaña, Sir?

PERIBAÑEZ: I am marching to Toledo;
   I'm ordered to lead these soldiers there.

The war carries us all away
but we keep you in the jealous care
of our hearts and memories.

CASILDA: You have no need of jealousy
if we are truly defended there.

PERIBAÑEZ: If I doubted that, then Lady,
I would not be leaving here.
Certainty is my only peace
as I leave to march as far away
as the end of this dark world.
I've come to say goodbye to you
in the strange speech of a gentleman.
Listen to me: who would have said
the peasant harvesting his fields
with the bright blade of his sickle,
or with his bare feet in the grapes
treading out the crimson juice,
or with his work-roughened hands
guiding the plough down the furrow,
would talk one day with a captain's voice,
and wear these presumptuous feathers
and carry this sword of knighthood?
But now I am a gentleman
since our Lord Comendador
with his own hands gave me this power.
And if it come to pass that I
need to use it, I will prove
the equal to that gentleman
in courage and in honour.
Now will you grant your Captain
some favour or trinket I can keep?

CASILDA: You are talking a strange language
which I do not understand.
As to the favour, what can I,
a village girl, give to a Captain?

PERIBAÑEZ: You must not lower yourself.

CASILDA: Take this black ribbon. The colour of war.

PERIBAÑEZ: This stands for grief and banishment.

BLAS: And you, my Lady Costanza,
won't you give me something too?

COSTANZA: Here, take this old bit of string
which I use to tie up my dog.
Since you're going to fight with dogs
you can use it in battle.

BLAS: May God make ribbons of my skin
if I don't kill the mongrels
as they retreat in terror.

INES: Nothing for yourself, Bartolo?

BARTOLO: Ines, as an old soldier
if not as a young lover,
you ought to give me something.

INES: So take this shoe.

BARTOLO: No, you keep it. From that height
it might prove a fatal gift.

INES: Then bring me home a real live Moor.

BARTOLO: I'll try, but they're hard men to catch;
if I don't bring you a live one
I'll recite the heroic story
of his capture in my own poetry.

*Enter LEONARDO as a captain, with drums and flag, and a
company of well-dressed GENTLEMEN.*

LEONARDO: March as ordered, gentlemen.

INES: Who are they?

COSTANZA: The gentlemens' lazy rabble.

INES: Our own men looked much sharper.

COSTANZA: These might be in fine uniforms
but their spirits don't look so bright.

LEONARDO: These country boys seem to believe
they can piss in our faces;
Let's demonstrate the proper way
to parade in a public place.

PERIBAÑEZ: Attention, men.
We'll show these gents a thing or two.

One company marches around the other, observing.

BLAS: Time to flaunt your gifts, Bartolo.

BARTOLO: Quiet! A noble spirit
makes up for my senile age.

LEONARDO: Listen; I don't like common men
competing with their betters.

BARTOLO: We'll see you on the battlefield.

BLAS: When they hear the screams of war
they'll turn and flee like frightened dogs.

BARTOLO: That's right; big words but cowards all.

The village troupe exits.

LEONARDO: Good, the peasants have gone.
Hey, Ines? Ines?

INES: Hello, is that my Captain calling?

LEONARDO: Why have both your cousins left?

INES: Surely you know why?
Everyone's miserable tonight.
Casilda's silent as a stone.

LEONARDO: Do you think perhaps there's a slight chance
> he could see her for a moment?

INES: Ssh, someone might be listening.
> I'll work out a way to let him in
> so she'll think it's Pedro coming home.

LEONARDO: If you really want to help me out
> blind that woman; she defends
> her honour far too carefully.
> Now our patience is running out;
> since yesterday the Comendador
> has resigned himself to death.

INES: Tell him to walk along the street.

LEONARDO: And the signal?

INES: A song.

LEONARDO: Good. Farewell.

INES: Will you be there?

LEONARDO: I'll leave the men in the charge
> of my second. I'll be there.

INES: Until later.

LEONARDO: March on men. Two suns have set.
> The day is growing dark.

Scene 3

The COMENDADOR in his house, dressed in ordinary clothes, with LUJAN his servant.

COMENDADOR: You saw him leaving town?

LUJAN: Yes, Sir.

COMENDADOR: You definitely saw him go?

LUJAN: On a fast mare, perfect for running away.
    If only you had seen him
    ordering his gang around –
    he's no competition, Sir.

COMENDADOR: His company is not unworthy.
    Yet I'd prefer his wife's, of course.

LUJAN: Who dares wins. So they say.

COMENDADOR: By tomorrow morning
    they'll be in Toledo for breakfast.

LUJAN: Depending on where they sleep tonight.

COMENDADOR: They won't halt before dawn, will they?

LUJAN: I doubt it. They're field-workers.
    They're used to it, and it's not far.
    The drum will keep them marching on
    all the way to Granada
    without a moment's rest,
    the distance growing ever further
    between him and Casilda.

COMENDADOR: What shall I do now?

LUJAN: What do you mean?

COMENDADOR: How can I wile away the hours
    between now and ten o'clock?

LUJAN: It's almost nine already.
    Why are you looking so sad?
    You've almost gained the victory!
    Think what a perfect chance this is!
    Grasp it while you can, and Hope
    will surely grant you your desire.

COMENDADOR: While my desire still eludes me,
    I must wait without hope.

LUJAN: Is Leonardo coming too?

COMENDADOR: Of course he is;
    he's promised to marry Ines,
    so she'll open the door tonight
    and let us in.

LUJAN: Is there a signal or something?

COMENDADOR: Music. A song.

LUJAN: What if they scare her away?

COMENDADOR: They'll provide our cover
    so we can slip in past the men.

LUJAN: A good plan.
    Did you hear about that wedding?
    All the family members
    had gathered from far and wide;
    the priest arrived on time,
    the groom, best man and bridesmaid
    were all dressed up and waiting;
    the musicians were ready to play;
    but when the bride appeared at last
    she said she was there against her will;
    and when the Priest said 'Do you?'
    she refused the man three times.
    The wedding was a disaster.

COMENDADOR: What are you trying to tell me?

LUJAN: You're pushing a rock uphill, Sir.
    Because she is so difficult
    you need her to say yes.

COMENDADOR: I've tried the soft and gentle way;
    now I'm forced to use force.
    Once I'm in her room tonight
    neither of us will have a choice.

LUJAN: Good may yet come out of this.
    But I think were walking into the dark.

Enter SERVANT and MUSICIANS.

SERVANT: The musicians are here, Sir.

1ST MUSICIAN: At your service until dawn, Sir.

COMENDADOR: Friends, I put my trust in you.
My honour is at stake tonight.

The church bells ring the hour.

COMENDADOR: How many times did it sound?

LUJAN: I thought it was ten.

COMENDADOR: The waiting is almost over.

LUJAN: Keep calm now, Sir. Are you hungry?

COMENDADOR: Of course I'm not hungry.

LUJAN: Well, drink something then.

COMENDADOR: Is it cold? Is there ice?

SERVANT: There's no ice Sir.

COMENDADOR: Then share it out between you.

SERVANT: I've brought your cloak Sir.

COMENDADOR: Show me.

SERVANT: The black one.

COMENDADOR: Is this some sort of stupid joke?
Why have you brought me mourning clothes?

SERVANT: Which one would you prefer, Sir?

LUJAN: The clandestine lover
never wears his brightest clothes.
They give too much away.

COMENDADOR: Give me the other, you idiot.

SERVANT: Here it is, Sir.

COMENDADOR: Goddess of Love, guide me now;
    may my long days of servitude
    win me one night of love.

LUJAN: Shall I come along with you?

COMENDADOR: Leonardo's still not here.
    Yes, everybody follow me
    including the musicians;
    perhaps your sweet, harmonious art
    will calm the fire in my heart.

Scene 4

The square in Ocaña.

PERIBAÑEZ: Thanks for a fast horse that can fly
    across the distances of night.
    I left my company of men
    and suddenly I am here again.
    Under the light of the harvest moon,
    under the turbulent stars above,
    in the fields I stopped and saw
    a silent graveyard of skeletons;
    rank upon rank of hollow stalks
    standing to attention, taller than men,
    heads dry and dead and withered, until
    the darkness moved and I heard them
    whispering my name
    and the joke of my dishonour.
    Then they stared at me and laughed.
    My own shadow drew me on
    up the white dust of the lane
    past houses shut and locked and still.
    No dogs barked. No night bird sang.
    My shadow grew along the walls
    and leaped across the empty square
    to fall upon what was my home.
    Somewhere I thought I heard music.

Here I stand before this door.
What now?

PERIBAÑEZ knocks on the door.

A small light comes on.

ANTON: Who is it?

PERIBAÑEZ: Anton –

ANTON: Pedro? What are you doing here?
    What time is it?

PERIBAÑEZ: Quickly. I need you to let me in.
    I want to use your side door
    to get into my house. Don't ask.
    I think you understood everything
    at the painter's shop in the city.

ANTON: What could I say? But Casilda –

PERIBAÑEZ: Is an angel. Yes, I know.

ANTON: Do you know what you are doing?

PERIBAÑEZ: Don't try to stop me. It is too late.
    My head is tight with fear and hate.

Scene 5

Enter the COMENDADOR and LUJAN with the SERVANT and MUSICIANS.

COMENDADOR: Start the music now.
    The breeze will carry your voices.

The MUSICIANS tune up.

COMENDADOR: Can't you just play the song?

MUSICIANS: We need to tune our instruments.

COMENDADOR: I hate it when they tune the strings.
Cacophony, no harmony.

MUSICIANS: (*Sing.*)
At your door, lady
I lay slain
you did not cry
God save you

On your wedding day
I was hurt
and I cried out
My lady

I am dying
for your love
God save you
my sweet lady

But at your door
my sweet lady
you do not cry
God save you

INES appears in the doorway.

INES: Be quiet! You'll wake the whole street.

COMENDADOR: Ines, I am in agony.
Don't make me wait. The time has come.
Pray for me.

INES: Where's Leonardo?

COMENDADOR: I don't know; he should be here.
Ines: guide me through this dark
labyrinth to my heart's desire,
my cold stone of love.

INES: Has Leonardo gone to Toledo?
He won't come back tonight, then;

he'll want to strut before the girls
in his decorated uniform,
the Captain in the big city.

COMENDADOR: Perhaps he's doing precisely that,
or perhaps he's dreaming in his bed.
It hardly matters. Let me in.

INES: So he's not coming after all.

LUJAN: I'm going in as well.

COMENDADOR: (*To the SERVANT and MUSICIANS.*)
Go home now. Here's money. Keep quiet.

*He leaves. The COMENDADOR, LUJAN and INES go into the
house.*

1ST MUSICIAN: So then. What shall we do now?

2ND MUSICIAN: Haven't we got any other work?

1ST MUSICIAN: Nothing until tomorrow night.

2ND MUSICIAN: I'm going home to bed, then.

1ST MUSICIAN: She's lovely.

2ND MUSICIAN: Yes. Nice. I'm jealous too.

1ST MUSICIAN: Ah well. Let's go.

Scene 6

PERIBAÑEZ enters his house.

PERIBAÑEZ: I climbed the orchard wall like a thief
to break into my own house, and found
the door to the yard unbolted.
I thought I could hide in the henhouse
but they'd start to fluster and crow,
hearing the blood beat in my head.
Moonlight filtered through the slats

and I saw the cockerel on his perch,
the gold king in his soft red crown,
dreaming off-guard among the hens.
Look at you, I whispered, asleep
when the fox is on the prowl
in his stink of heat and lust,
craning his red neck in the dark:
two eyes of fire observing you.
How can you sleep when I'm awake
with this tangled panic in my head?
I curse the day that stranger came;
our lives were simple and happy;
he's like a splinter in our hearts.
Christ, these are tears on my face.
Now is the moment of revenge.
Voices: I must hide. He thinks
I am miles away from home.

He hides.

Enter CASILDA and INES.

CASILDA: I'm sure I heard someone out here.

INES: Don't be silly.

CASILDA: You were talking to a man.

INES: Who, me?

CASILDA: Yes, you.

INES: What did you hear?

CASILDA: If it wasn't you I heard
    then it must be thieves.

INES: Thieves?

CASILDA: Shout for help

INES: No!

CASILDA: Then I will.

INES: No, don't. You'll wake the street.
It's all in your imagination.

Enter the COMENDADOR and LUJAN.

COMENDADOR: Casilda. I am in love with you
and my heart cannot stay silent.
Since the day you saved my life
I have adored each part of you,
your face, your brow, your lips, your eyes;
in my loneliness I drink
the dark wine of your memory.
But the time has come for my release;
only you can grant me peace.
I am the Comendador.
I am your lord and master.

CASILDA: My husband is my only lord.
You are not my master. Sir.

COMENDADOR: I stand here as your willing slave
but I am still your master.
Either take pity on my pain
or I will expose you publicly
and say I found you with this man.

CASILDA: So cousin, you have betrayed me.

INES: Don't be so melodramatic;
we know each other better than that.
You're just a village girl like me,
married to a local man,
an ordinary farmer.
Now you should be sensible.
We both know the facts of life.
So does every village wife:
our beauty lasts until we marry;
say no and you will soon be sorry.
Remember, the Comendador,

a man of wealth, status and power,
risks more danger being here,
honouring your lowly house,
than you do from his presence.
Your honour is a quaint device;
forget it quickly, and embrace
this gentleman and his desire.
No-one else will ever know;
this is a secret between us now.

CASILDA: God forgive you. I will not.
I trusted you. The go-between;
the pimp that makes of me a whore.

COMENDADOR: Get out now. Leave us alone.

LUJAN: Come on, let's go.
They'll work it out in private.

LUJAN and INES exit.

COMENDADOR: It is pointless to refuse.
Whatever you do, you will lose.
I asked you gently, like a lover;
now I'll take you like a soldier.

CASILDA: You are the Lord of Ocaña
but I am the wife of a Captain.
If you try to touch me again
I will tear your eyes out.

COMENDADOR: Come on, there is no need to cry.

PERIBAÑEZ: (*Aside.*) What am I? A simple farmer
hiding in my own house –
or a man of honour
standing in the shadows
to declare my revenge?
This is the moment he must die.
Here I am, Comendador.
Forgive me, Sir. For all your power
the honour of this act is mine.

He drives his sword into the COMENDADOR's chest.

COMENDADOR: You have killed me. Pity me.

PERIBAÑEZ: Don't be afraid. Come quickly.

CASILDA: I cannot speak.

They exit into the dark. The COMENDADOR collapses into a chair.

COMENDADOR: Christ's blood.
God have mercy.
What have I done?
You give me this last moment of life
to beg forgiveness for my sin
from the man who is my subject.

Enter LEONARDO.

LEONARDO: Sir? Oh Jesus – this is blood –

COMENDADOR: Listen. Do not seek revenge.
It is too late, and I was wrong.
He was right to murder me.
I need to make confession.
And I pardon Peribañez.

LEONARDO: Not seek revenge?
He will writhe on the point of my sword
like the peasant dog he is.

COMENDADOR: He is no peasant.
He is a man of true honour.
I made him a gentleman,
and gave him the sword which takes my life
and he has used it truthfully.

LEONARDO: I'll find a Doctor. You won't die.

COMENDADOR: This place is dark. I need more light.

They exit.

Enter PERIBAÑEZ and CASILDA, LUJAN and INES.

PERIBAÑEZ: Prepare to die.

INES: I am already dead.
Spare me –

LUJAN: Please don't do this –

PERIBAÑEZ: But I must. Now is the time.

LUJAN: Why?

PERIBAÑEZ: Because of what you are.
A liar.
Betrayer of my own home.

INES: And me? And me?

PERIBAÑEZ: Reward for all your treachery.

He strikes them both.

LUJAN: He's stabbed me.

INES: Casilda – help me –

LUJAN and INES exit.

PERIBAÑEZ: They're lying in the doorway.

CASILDA: They deserved their punishment.

PERIBAÑEZ: Will you come away with me?

CASILDA: I am yours again, come what may.

PERIBAÑEZ: We need to get far away tonight.
Ride through the dark into daylight.
And then decide what to do.

CASILDA: God take the Comendador.
I have no pity for his soul;
his lust and privilege and power
led him to his death. Farewell.

They exit.

Scene 7

The KING's palace in Toledo. Enter KING ENRIQUE and the CONSTABLE.

KING: This is excellent, Constable.
    It delights my heart to see
    how joyfully all Castile
    has joined with my campaign.

CONSTABLE: They hate the Moorish kings, Sire.

KING: Andalucia must be free
    before the coming winter.
    Juan de Velasco, I charge you
    to display my several armies
    on the plains below the city
    so that the wide world may behold
    from these ancient walls of stone
    how pavilions, tents and armour
    rise up like a new Toledo
    radiant in the sunlight.
    Let the Moor hide in Granada
    before the sight of our power,
    as our numberless armies
    march like a forest of red flags
    raising dust across the plains.
    Where once he laughed, he'll weep
    and beg for mercy on his knees.

CONSTABLE: I'll marshal the men at once.

KING: Here comes the Queen.
    I adore her. Her presence
    always inspires my fighting men.

Enter the QUEEN and her LADIES IN WAITING.

QUEEN: Are you occupied my Lord?
    I can come back later.

KING: No, you're always welcome. Stay.
You know I value your sound advice
on the great matters of war and peace.
How is our son, the little prince?

QUEEN: He cries because you are not there.

KING: The good Lord save him; in his face
we trace the royal lineaments
of men far greater than I.

QUEEN: He is your son. He does not need
any further flattery.

KING: And as he is also your son
so he inherits your virtues too.

QUEEN: Poor child, he is not old enough
to fight beside you in this war.

KING: One day he will defend Christ's name.

Enter GOMEZ MANRIQUE.

KING: What are those drums?

GOMEZ: The troops of Estremadura and La Vera.

CONSTABLE: And Guadalajara and Atienza next.

KING: And the Ocaña men?

GOMEZ: They've been delayed.
Those who have already arrived
bring bad news, Sire.
They tell a story of murder;
a peasant in Ocaña
has murdered Don Fadrique
brutally, in cold blood.

KING: Fadrique? The greatest soldier
ever to wear the cross of a knight?

QUEEN: Is this true?

GOMEZ: It is certain.

KING: This is tragic news.
    What happened?

GOMEZ: Jealousy, Sire.

KING: Justified?

GOMEZ: Of course not, Sire. There was no cause.

QUEEN: Jealousy respects no law.

KING: Has the murderer been caught?

GOMEZ: No; on the night of the foul deed
    he fled the town with his young wife.

QUEEN: What is the peasant's name?

GOMEZ: His name is Peribañez, Mam.
    They say he was an honourable man.

KING: This is a truly shameful thing.
    That I should have to hear such news
    on an important day like this.
    Is this how Spain truly respects
    the laws and justice of the King?
    Make proclamations in the cities
    and in Ocaña too;
    The King offers a thousand crowns
    for the murderer, alive or dead.
    Any man who shelters him
    or assists his escape in any way
    does so on pain of instant death.

GOMEZ: The announcement will be made.

    He exits.

KING: The heavens will not hide this man.

QUEEN: He'll soon be discovered:
    the promise of gold works wonders.

KING: A peasant who dares to murder
    a great knight of our kingdom
    shall not escape my justice.
    I swear I shall make this killer
    an example to the people.

Enter PAGE.

PAGE: A labourer attends outside.
    He says he needs to speak to you
    regarding matters of great weight
    and importance to the Campaign.

KING: Let him be admitted.

Enter PERIBAÑEZ dressed as a worker, with CASILDA.

KING: (*To QUEEN.*) My dear. Let us be seated. Approach.

PERIBAÑEZ: My lord, allow me to kiss your feet.

KING: Get up off your knees and speak.

PERIBAÑEZ: How can I speak? The power of speech
    has failed me in your presence.
    But since I must, I speak these words
    in the confidence of your justice.
    My name is Peribañez.

KING: Then you shall die. Guards, kill him now.

QUEEN: Not in my presence. Hold him.

PERIBAÑEZ: Enrique the Just, why must I die
    before you listen to my story?

QUEEN: I think he is correct, my Lord.
    Perhaps you should hear him.

KING: Indeed, indeed. The testimony
    of both sides should always be heard.
    Speak.

PERIBAÑEZ: I am a man, a country man,

of the old blood of this ancient land.
I was the first among my equals
who gave me the deciding vote
on all matters of importance.
I was mayor for six years.
I married this woman. She too
is of good blood, a country girl;
virtuous, and without envy.
But on our wedding day
the Comendador of Ocaña,
our Lord, fell in love with her.
Pretending thanks for some service
we had simply rendered him,
he gave me some fine tapestries
with which to decorate our house.
I confess I was too pleased
with these unnecessary riches
and the pride of his attention,
for the price was my dishonour.
One night I was away from home,
he broke in to seduce my wife;
but he was foiled; she locked him out.
When I returned and heard of this
I tore his hangings from my walls.
I knew from then what he wanted.
But he called me to his house
to tell me your gracious majesty
had commanded him to gather men
to serve you in the new campaign.
He made me Captain of a troop
of one hundred of the village men
and set me marching to the war
away from Ocaña and my wife.
But I foresaw my honour
would be lost to me for ever;
so I rode back to town that night.

What did I find? The door open wide,
and my wife powerless in his hands.
I cried for justice, drew my sword
and ran him through his perjured heart.
We fled away into the dark
not knowing where to turn for truth;
and in Toledo I discovered
the high price set upon my head.
I told my wife to bring me here
and offer myself up to you.
Have pity on her; when I die
give her the reward.

KING: Well?

QUEEN: I weep for him. My tears prove
    his act was valour, and for love.

KING: This is all highly unusual:
    a peasant valuing his reputation!
    But he was made a gentleman
    by the Comendador himself,
    and has performed courageously
    to defend his honour and his wife's;
    therefore let the country hear:
    I grant him, by my grace, his life.
    This is the work of justice.
    And I require a brave Captain
    to lead the men on this campaign.
    Give the money to his wife.
    And henceforth you are granted
    the right to bear my royal arms.

PERIBAÑEZ: You are worthy of your justice, Sire.

QUEEN: And I would like to give to you,
    most true and honoured wife,

dresses to suit the lovely lady
of a Captain of the King.

KING and QUEEN: Well, my dear. An extraordinary story.

They exit.

EPILOGUE

PERIBAÑEZ: Casilda. Do you remember all the words
    we chose for our love alphabets?
    Now I only have one word
    and I have learned its truth by heart:
    but I can hardly say it.

CASILDA: Once upon a time, on our wedding day,
    you wanted to give me all the world;
    a river like a silver ring,
    a town of bright gold on a hill,
    a dress made of the first spring sky,
    and a crown of the moon and stars.
    It was a picture from a book.

    Now all I want is to go home,
    if somewhere you can find this place;
    where the birds whistle and call,
    and the fountain runs simple and clean,
    and the day turns in its circle,
    and the night is for the story
    of our heartbeats, you and I.

    The End.

WWW.OBERONBOOKS.COM

CPSIA information can be obtained
at www.ICGtesting.com
Printed in the USA
LVHW081312301219
642066LV00014B/971/P

9 780948 230660